A BLAC

SPEAKS

CHERRY SCOTT

CHERRY ENTERPRISES
*

1

Library of Congress Catalog
Card Number: 92-075860

ISBN 0-9635182-0-8

Printed in the United States of America

First Edition

Cover Photo By Al Germany

Edited by Odell Johnson

FORWARD

To all the people that I have ever met in my
lifetime, as well as those that I have not...this
book is for you.   In 1992 as America
experiences national devastation in the areas
of violent crime, poverty, unemployment,
physical abuse, police brutality, aids, child
neglect/abuse, illiteracy, racial disharmony
and death of the American Dream, "A Black
Woman Speaks" is my personal contribution
toward the betterment of man/womankind as ,
we *all* must lend a hand in healing the wounds
that stifle, stagnate, strangle and destroy the
rights of all for peace, prosperity, happiness,
justice, freedom and liberty.

As a thirty-six year old, experienced black
woman, I am old enough to understand the
moods, philosophies, attitudes, prejudices and
beliefs of American people that contribute to
the problems that plague us all.   Yet I am
young enough to realize that there is hope,
whereas many Americans feel hopeless and
helpless in their quests and desires to attain
satisfying living standards that promote
personal growth, economic security and equal
opportunities.

Hopeful and positive, I wholeheartedly feel
that America--*the land of the free and the
home of the brave* can be transformed into a
"utopia" of sorts. (an ideally perfect place) I
truly believe that the American dream can be
restored, but first, all Americans must join
together to eliminate poverty, unemployment,
violent crime, illiteracy, racial disharmony,
ghettos, self-defeat and self destruction.

But before we can join together to achieve
anything for all people we must come together

3

in an effort to communicate and understand one another regardless of race, sex, age or nation of origin. All Americans must strive to educate themselves and others about all that America stands for and means i.e., racial diversity, values, peace, morals, democracy, justice, prosperity and equal opportunities to all pursuits of happiness.

We all must strive to change the mindset of Americans. The mindset of America must be changed from negative to positive because it is in the hearts and minds of Americans where the American Dream has turned into a nightmare. Thus Americans have withdrawn within themselves to shield themselves from the harsh realities of honesty and truth about themselves and others.

Thus it is within the inner-turmoil in each and every one of us that frustration, depression, confusion, anger, guilt, insecurity, jealousy, self-hate, ignorance and racial hatred festers and explodes as lying, cheating, stealing, robbing, killing, child abuse, spousal abuse, violent crime, discrimination, racism, sexism, sexual harassment and police brutality. These are the painful tragedies that destroy us all a little everyday. Hence, leaving us all with one question..."why?"

The American dream has turned into a nightmare because of our inabilities to deal with frustration, anger and pain. "A Black Woman Speaks" was written to address all the anger, frustration, confusion, hate and pain that I have felt seen or heard in my thirty-six years. And if I have been exposed to it, I know that you have too. I see that the problem lies in the fact that no one wants to deal with all the hurt, frustration and pain. But as we approach the twenty-first century, American problems are too big to ignore. There is time to make a fresh start in 1993. With a new President, (Clinton) a new attitude and a will to succeed, all Americans should take advantage of this chance to make a difference for the better.

We must realize that it is not each other that we dislike or even hate, it is the things that we do that causes so much misery and pain. "A Black Woman Speaks" lays the pain on the table for all to see just how ugly and unnecessary poverty, hate, illiteracy, crime, violence, unemployment and racism really is. "A Black Woman Speaks" is my attempt and ongoing commitment to bridge the gaps between the races, the ages, the rich and the poor, the loved and the unloved, the educated and uneducated. "A Black Woman Speaks" is an outpouring of love from you to me that should spread throughout humanity to heal the wounds of all in America and around the world.

To the truth...
until you face it
head on
and face forward
you shall forever and always remain
a prisoner to you pain!

TABLE OF CONTENTS

Page

CHAPTER ONE

THE BLACK WOMAN
...HER TRIALS, TRIBULATIONS AND TRIUMPHS

The black female that grows up to be a black woman....Who is she and why? A mystery to most...why is she so misunderstood by her children, her man and society at large? She feels she is different from what we perceive her to be...is she and why? What is her place in America...does she have a place in America? What is the problem between the black woman, the black man and the children they raise? What is to become of her...her children...her man... her family...her race? Just who IS that black woman in America?

The black woman living in America is a collage of the entire human race...from Africa to Europe, to Asia and then to America. The black woman in America, descended from Africa, many centuries ago, is the past, present and future of the universe. The black woman is all that we were, all that we are and all that we will ever be, no more, no less. Only the truth will set you free. To know the truth, to accept the truth, to live the truth, is where you shall find joy, success and peace of mind.

The black woman in America is strong, weak, rich, poor, brilliant, illiterate, funny, sad, soft, hard, wise, shallow, successful and oppressed. The bloodlines of the black woman in America tie into practically every known nationality around the world.

The black woman in America has a skin tone that spans from smooth, deep, dark chocolate, to smooth, creamy vanilla. The hair of the black woman ranges from tight, tiny curls to long, flowing tresses. The American black woman's eyes span from a rainbow of hues, as well, from deep, misty, black to vibrant, coral green. Undeniable, the beauty of the black woman, unappreciated and overlooked for far too long, is a precious resource that must be rediscovered as yet, another great and mystical wonder of the world.

FROM the times of ancient history, that brought us the beautiful, black Egyptian, Queen Nefertari described as a Negress of great beauty...strong personality and remarkable administrative ability.

TO Harriet Tubman, (a woman called Moses) an anti-slavery activist who between 1850 and 1860 traveled back and forth from the South and the North, (much of the way on foot) 19 times to guide over 300 blacks, including her parents to freedom. The black woman has been a savior, a leader, a teacher, an entertainer and a mother to us all.

TO Josephine Baker, born in 1906, a celebrated beautiful black woman who ventured to Paris, France. Escaping grinding poverty, Josephine Baker become an overwhelming success as an entertainer, a pilot and a secret agent during World War II. More than an entertainer, Josephine Baker was one of the first crusaders for black civil rights. In 1954, at the age of 48, the courageous woman called Josephine Baker adopted 12 children of different nationalities, to show the world that there is such a thing as a universal family.

TO Vanessa Williams, the first black woman to be crowned Miss America. Though suffering a misfortune Vanessa Williams, rose again as a movie star and singer, selling 800,000 copies of her first recording album and appearing on the cover of Harper's Bazaar Magazine (June of 1992) as one of America's 10 Most Beautiful women.

AND to Oprah Winfrey, who at the age of 15 wrote "I just want to be the best person I can be" rising to hold the spot of best television talk show host of 1992, a millionaire, surpassing many others as she strengthens the lines of communication in cities across America, between all races to discussing topics of concern to millions. More than a millionaire, Oprah Winfrey topped the list for Forbes' highest paid entertainers in 1992, earning 42 million dollars.

The black woman is an untapped resource, a timeless treasure, a vital link between the success and failure of mankind--the human race.

Of these distinctions and accomplishments, all black females/women around the world must realize and embrace the value of who the black woman is and who the black woman is destined to become--the essence and future of the universe. The young and beautiful black female, growing up to become a beautiful black woman must love, preserve, value, enhance and cherish her beauty as a precious gift and honor. For the black woman holds a very esteemed position in the birth and survival of ALL mankind.

For the benefit of the human race, all other females must allow themselves to appreciate and respect the beauty of the black female for it is the black female's beauty that provides the uniqueness of all the other beautiful women of the world. Males, regardless of race, color or creed, must respect, value, protect and preserve the black female as one would a

valuable, fragile work of art. The black woman
is the mother of all mankind--our past, our
present and our future. The black woman aids
in giving that which is most important to us--
life. To the black woman, we must be thankful,
respectful and appreciative, as we should be to
all women, regardless of race, age or nation of
origin.

The black female in America possesses a
personality and spirit to compliment her
diverse physical appearance. A black woman
easily situates herself to effectively adjust to
the surroundings of her environment,
regardless of the setting. The black woman, a
part of all that we know and feel, can feel
comfortable and relaxed with welfare
recipients, but in an instant can stand firm
and tall among those in socioeconomic or
intellectual levels, equal or higher than her
own. The black female readily finds play time
for a bubbly two year old, quiet understanding
for the confused adolescent and compassion for
the elderly. The black female is sensitive and
keenly perceptive. The basic core of a black
woman's nature is loving and compassionate.

The black female in America has changed and
is constantly changing in many ways from the
first African woman to arrive in America 113
years before the birth of George Washington
(the first President of the United States) and
244 years before the signing of the
Emancipation Proclamation (1863).

The history of the black woman, from Africa,
in America began in August of 1619 with a
woman named Isabella. Establishing the
merchandising and marketing of human
beings, the slave trade began with a black
woman. The black woman from Africa existed
as a part of slavery that started in 1444 and

continued for over 400 years. With slavery as a painful memory and historical backdrop, the black woman in America, with ancestors from Africa, is the epitome of fortitude, determination, strength, pride and will to survive. Still struggling to survive in the nineties, the black woman helped build the greatest country in the world through blood, sweat, tears and no pay at all.

Beyond the pain, the black woman is an intricate part of the American culture. Constantly changing, sometimes leading, sometimes following, the black woman easily adapts to the ways of America, the black race and the race of all mankind, the human race. Surviving the pain, the black woman, adapts, changes and grows to continue her struggles in coping with the trials and tribulations of surviving in America. As life is not an easy task for anyone, be they rich, poor, black or white, life is much more challenging for a woman who is black, but determined to succeed.

The history of blacks in American dictated that black women be strong, intelligent, aggressive and independent, throughout much of their entire lives. The black woman's mood is emotional, compassionate, soft, with strong desires to be loved and comforted as she copes with womanhood and the uniqueness of her black beauty in America. Restless, frustrated and impatient as a result of being misunderstood, separated and alienated from that which she is very much a part, the black woman may often show signs of anger, ruthlessness and reckless abandon as she seeks to overcome the obstacles that stand between her and racial equality, understanding and her own definition of personal dignity, respect and success.

Regardless of her strength, the black woman would like to rely on the men of America and other countries for maintaining peace, strength, security and leadership for the survival of the human race. The black woman looks first to the black man for he is her racial counterpart. But, as fate would have it, the black male has fallen short of being the leader, the father figure for the black race. Thus, the black woman is forced to compensate for the absence, inadequacy and deficiency, of the black male.

As the black woman learned to compensate for what the black male does not do as a man for the black race, the black male in America continues to weaken, while the black woman becomes stronger in her quest for survival and success in America. In many, cases it is the success of the black female that serves to separate the black male from the black female. Strangely it is the strengthening of black womanhood that contributes to the weakening of black manhood.

Up until the seventies, it was a rarity for great numbers of black women to become successful in areas outside of the family structure. A wide variety of career choices and opportunities were not always the norm for the American black woman, though "work" has always been a common way of life for the average black woman in America. Having a family and maintaining the love and strength of the family structure was once a satisfying reward for the black woman. The family was the duty, responsibility and most often, ultimate goal in life for the black woman.

In like fashion, it was the black man's responsibility, duty and ultimate goal in life to feed, clothe and provide shelter for his wife

13

and children. When men were men, whatever a man did for his family was cause for celebration, appreciation and reverence. The family was once the essence of life for black men, women and children. But much has changed in the roles of manhood and womanhood since the 1950's.

By the early eighties, roles, responsibilities, goals, values, morals and circumstances changed dramatically, drastically for American men and women regardless of race. Very much a part of the American social structure, black women took advantage of the positive changes. All women, black and white began to gain rights and opportunities allowing them to become active in the mechanism of further social change, progress and upward mobility.

Society, having lowered and eased the barriers that alienated and oppressed blacks and women, society became less focused on the maintenance of racial and sexual discrimination, oppression and segregation. Doors once closed to women and blacks begin to open for anyone eager for positive changes, social mainstreaming, integration, opportunities and improved living standards.

Having been primarily relegated to responsibilities of home and family, black and white women alike found personal satisfaction in their newly available opportunities to become a functional part of society, once controlled and dominated by men. Men and women could not altogether handle their newfound opportunities to succeed, prosper and grow. The family structure in America died a slow death as America grew as a super, modern, power of the world.

The following chart shows how men and women, (black and white) have carelessly become parents. And in that carelessness, Americans themselves have weakened the strength of the traditional family structure. Blacks show to be more careless than whites as their percentages for out-of-wedlock births far outnumber that of whites.

PERCENTAGE OF OUT-OF-WEDLOCK BIRTHS
1950-1988

	BLACK	WHITE
1950	16.8%	1.7%
1960	21.6%	2.3%
1970	37.6%	5.7%
1980	56.4%	9.3%
1988	63.7%	14.9%

For reasons unknown millions of American men, black and white have grown careless in the sustaining of American dreams and quality living standards for themselves and the children they father. As a result women, black and white have been forced to compensate in the home and in the workplace. Women, now aware that males will not and can not always step up to their responsibilities as fathers or husbands, must consider the well-being of children when circumstances are unlikely to be in the best interest of young, innocent children. No child deserves to live in poverty.

In reading an article in the January 1992, issue of Cosmopolitan entitled, "When You're Doing Better Than He Is" by Michael Barson, the article seems to suggest that the male success factor is often reduced when compared to his female counterpart. This article further confirms that the problems of "tradition" relative to men and women, in the nineties, is a problem that crosses racial barriers.

Though a great number of males can be heard to say that they want women who are successful, bright and socially aggressive, their actions usually prove otherwise as figures rise in male unemployment rates, absent fathers, prison populations and male welfare recipients. Resulting in a mutual problem between males and females, all of society is negatively affected when success is tipped in the woman's favor, especially if the woman is black. Many males of the nineties still feel that women with children should remain in the home with the children, holding home and family as primary concern and interest.

No longer traditional, many women of the nineties, black and white, place a great deal of importance on personal education, careers, politics as well as on other social issues of which they feel compelled to promote change. Having not yet learned to fully accept progress and growth in people, places and things, society allows negativity to oftentimes outweigh the advantages of positive productivity and change.

In the nineties, pain and suffering is still quite prevalent within the black race, though it is in large part self-inflicted. Blacks refuse to realize or admit that many of the problems that plague the black race are problems caused by blacks themselves. Some blacks who feel that they have "arrived" oftentimes separate themselves from the essence of who they are. All blacks are people descended from Africa with common bloodlines, common pain, common suffering, common accomplishments and strides. A major problem that exists (in the nineties) between the black male and female evolve out of their beliefs and behavior that suggests that there is no longer a real need to feel any type of racial, social or family bond between the black man and black woman outside of romantic, family or friendship ties. Though common bonds do exist within the black race, they are weak and fragmented as blacks have let die their pride and loyalty to one another as members of the black race. The interest that black women have shown in matters outside of the black male and the black family to survive and grow has served to further separate black males and females.

Though all blacks should be able to benefit from the advancement of black women in the areas of educational and economical advancements, black males shy away from black females who concern themselves with personal growth, advancement and self-improvement. Rather than using the advancement of black women as a foundation for further advancement of the black race, black males ignore, overlook and sometimes set out to destroy the most valuable resource available to them--the ambitious black woman.

One might ask, why should black males be re-uniting with the black woman, utilizing her strength, beauty and intelligence? Simple, the black woman became strong as a result of the independence that was forced upon her by black males who abandoned black women. The black male in America separated himself from the black female as he sought fun and frolic. Unfortunately, the black male's fun has resulted in the demise, destruction and a rampant death rate of black males in America as the twenty-first century approaches.

Dating back more than fifty years ago, black males were then unable to cope with the talents and ambitions of beautiful, strong black woman. Lena Horne, one of the most beautiful and talented black women of our times, labeled as tall, tan and terrific, suffered from the insecurities of a man unable to cope with black beauty, intelligence and ambition. Lena Horne, in 1937 married a man who expected her to be a homemaker--ironing shirts, cooking meals and leaving financial affairs to her husband, though she was accustomed to handling more money than he had ever seen. By her husband, Lena Horne was expected to be excluded from discussions of politics and social issues. Bored with housework, Lena Horne much preferred intelligent conversation. Obviously not open to teamwork, upward mobility, personal achievement and the support of an ambitious, beautiful, black woman, Lena Horne's husband voiced his opposition to her career forcing Lena Horne to become intent on ending her marriage.

The ambitious black female in America is naturally inclined to consistently increase and enhance her strengths and resources as a result of institutionalized slavery that became her lot in life for over 400 years. (Growth is what life is all about anyway. When any form of life ceases to grow, death is soon to come.) Black female slaves, forced to endure much hardship and pain, relied on their inner strengths as the slave family was very fragile within the black society of slavery. The slave family in America had no legal rights and black marriages had no standing in law. At any point in time the husband, wife or children of a slave union could be separated by sale to other slave owners, separating family members, sometimes forever.

In that blacks fought to receive equal, human rights as individuals and families, black women feel intense disappointment, resentment and anger toward black males who willingly disregard and devalue the bonds between the black family structure, black females, black children and most other members of the black race.

Motivated by a strong will, black females remain flexible in their candor accepting most or all of that which is offered or given. Situations or circumstances unacceptable to black females tend to strengthen their energies to transpose negative situations into positive, more acceptable situations. To her advantage, the black woman attempts to make the most of her possessions and experiences regardless of how useless or irrelevant they may appear at the time. One of the black female's most valuable possessions is her education, be it formal or informal.

Black females, though formally educated in standard educational institutions, must also heavily rely on the educations that they receive outside of formal classroom settings. As a black person in America strives toward above average success, they are forced to function within a mainstream society that is predominantly regulated, operated and owned by white males. Blacks are primarily shut out from the benefits of mainstream America because black males have not yet learned how to organize and work in team efforts to acquire basic economic strength and power to help black race as a whole gain economic stability and security.

Moreover, blacks in and around Africa, such as Soweto Somalia and Haiti, continue to suffer with no relief because blacks in America can offer them no refuge. Most American nationalities, the Koreans, the Jews, the Russians, the Arabs, build businesses and social structures that can absorb their brothers and sisters from their homelands. Blacks however, are too involved in recreational activity to even consider that they are in large part to blame for the continued suffering of blacks around the world, oppressed and degraded by war and those who consider blacks, less than human.

Because of the black female's position in society and easy going spirit she is not seen as the threat that black males often pose to others. Racial harmony in American between whites and blacks has not been reached to adequately accommodate comfortable, common and equally available living standards. Though blacks and whites live, work and play together, they do not fully accept, understand and respect one another at a level that would promote racial harmony that would lead to the elimination of many of the problems that plague both white and black races as well as other races that live and function in America.

Because of the black female's perceived position in American society as mother, teacher, professional, social servant and sex object, valuable knowledge and experience flows easily and naturally to her. Some black males may harbor resentment toward black females because they feel that black females are more readily and easily accepted into mainstream society simply because of gender and the factors that characterize the make-up of females in general. It is quite possible that black females *are* more easily mainstreamed within the family educational institutions, the workforce and society.

Black females are able to acquire higher levels of maturity, wisdom and life experiences, at a much more accelerated rate when compared to black males. Most black females mature to an effective, basic adult level of understanding, rational and reasoning beginning as early as age sixteen. Because black females are afforded an edge in social acceptability and accessibility, even more reason is provided as to why black males should gravitate *toward* black females, rather than away from them if they are to survive and cease their own demise.

At the onset of adulthood, black females receive informal educational tools in almost all aspects of their lives. Of great benefit is the fact that black females may date males four to even twenty years older than themselves. Even if dating situations do not occur, black females are more apt to establish friendships of substance with older males wherein they are taught and guided to adopt attitudes and behavior patterns that will benefit them later in life. Black females gain valuable life experiences significantly earlier than their black male counterparts.

By contrast, if young black males gravitate toward older individuals, it is usually another black male. Though mentoring and big brother type organizations are in place to provide black males with positive role models, too often, informal black male instruction and guidance centers around sexual encounters and conquests that young black males are led to believe will define their manhood. Causing further harm to black males are the older black females who befriend young black males, subjecting them to sexual encounters that they are not mentally ready for.

21

Adding to the problem of absent fathers within the black race, some black females allow themselves to become pregnant by young males who could almost be labeled as innocent bystanders, disadvantaged by youth and inexperience. Herein black females contribute to the tragedies that pathetically harm the black race and the black family.

As young adult black males select their mates, they usually enter into relationships with females who are likely to be up to four years younger. Some thirty to forty year old males may choose mates that may be up to ten years younger. Because it is not the norm for black males to reach economic and intellectual maturity by the ages of thirty, they usually couple themselves with mates who offer very little that can lead to quality living standards as most young females do not possess the mindset of strength necessary to get and keep a black male focused on productivity, personal growth and quality living standards.

Recreational activity, the primary focus of far too many young black males, young black females are often pulled into the same dead end mindsets and ruts as young black couples set themselves up for a lifetime of ignorance, alienation, poverty and self-inflicted social oppression. A significant imbalance is thereby created between black females and black males simply as a result of the company they choose to keep. Not heard enough in the black community is the statement, "If it is your desire to become successful, one must surround one's self with successful people and others who also want and work toward success."

Partial explanation is thus established for a another circumstance that serves to further alienate the black male from the black female that adds to the lack of cohesion among members of the entire black race. "Together they stand--Divided they Fall."

As young black males gain experience and maturity, they may eventually gravitate toward black females who they perceive as equally mature and experienced. Between the ages of twenty-five to thirty-five, black males approach the point where they are ready to form healthy, mutually satisfying and purposeful relationships. However, it is often difficult for black males to accept the advanced maturity level of ambitious, socially aware and self assured black females. When black females try to bring black males up to an acceptable level of intelligence and social awareness, black males, ignorantly, take the stance, "no woman is going to change me."

In observing a black female, one should see a person who presents herself with an obvious air of confidence, poise and calm. The black woman is often looked upon as a person with whom a person can comfortably and confidentially confide. Open-minded and flexible, black females are usually open to new experiences and opportunities. Herein, the black female is further educated in areas and on subjects that she has not sought to obtain. Almost always aware of the difficulties that she must face everyday in her status as a black woman who seeks to attain quality living standards, the black female is eager and willing to learn about all that life is about, past, present and future.

The black female intentionally places herself in positions to become exposed to circumstances and situations that may be foreign to her own personal life and environment. Subconsciously, she realizes that there may come a time when foreign information, to her immediate black environment may be very useful, so she listens and learns with earnest concern and interest. Early in life, the black female learns that there is valuable education in all life experiences, circumstances and situation.

The black woman seems to instinctively realize that life will not always be easy for her, thus the smart black female prepares herself for the road ahead, early in life by surrounding herself with positive influence and resourceful knowledge. The black woman learns about compassion from the strong relationship of mother and child. The single black woman will often realize, that as a parent she may be her child's only hope and chance for survival. The black woman learns about sensitivity as she watches a baby born into poverty, growing up in poverty, living in poverty, only to die in poverty. Regardless of where the blame may lie for a life filled with hardship and pain, black women can usually relate to the sometimes "seemingly" unsurmountable obstacles that can destroy forever all hopes and dreams in a life of darkness and despair.

From a close or distant range, the black female learns the art of being shrewd from that which is ambiguous, seen but not shown, heard but not spoken. Experience and natural instincts allow the black female to read what is written in between the lines of the written word where the actual messages usually lie. Home to a great many young black females, the ghetto serves as the homeroom in the school of life for many black females where she learns some of her most valuable lessons to be used in overcoming all the obstacles that she is

24

destined to face as a black woman in a world dominated primarily by whites and or males.

The black female learns about <u>financial management</u> when she realizes that she must do with $100 what another person does with $500 or $1,000. The black female learns to be <u>strong</u> when she realizes that she may have to turn the other cheek in order to keep that which she has worked very hard to obtain. Though often forgiving for the wrongs that she must suffer, the black female is forever mindful of the respect that she knows that she deserves and seeks as an adult, as a woman, and essential member of the human race. Overtaken by anger, if a black female chooses not to turn the other cheek at the wrong moment, she learns the difference between foolish pride and healthy, justified pride.

The black female, sadly accepts and learns about <u>goals</u> and <u>aspirations</u> when she realizes that there may be no black male "knight in shining armor" as childhood fairytales led her to believe. She learns about <u>worldliness</u> from her attention to society and how it is presented via, the written word, television, live entertainment, interaction with those from different cultures and other social backgrounds.

The black female learns about female <u>self-worth</u> and <u>self-respect</u> when she is given or offered something of monetary value, usually from a male, as an expression of desire to get to know her better or as an expression of appreciation for a good deed that she has done. The experienced black woman learns about personal <u>dignity</u> when she realizes the consequences of her actions may not always be worth the momentary pleasure or gain, thus squelching the possibility for sexual harassment, abuse or unwelcome advantage.

The black female learns to be <u>humble</u> as she realizes the disadvantages of posing as a threat to those who may hold the keys to the doors that she needs to enter. The black female easily acquires a <u>sympathetic heart</u> as she realizes that the pain and suffering of others could easily be her own as blacks as a race of people, willingly live and function so closely to the thresholds of pain, misery, despair, hardship, poverty and almost everything with negative connotations or consequences. Sensitivity prompts the black woman to learn about <u>diplomacy</u> when she finds it absolutely necessary to relay troublesome information, but wants to keep a relationship on solid, stable ground.

Fortunate black females, lucky or smart enough to learn necessary social skills by the age of thirteen, fourteen or fifteen able to move toward young adulthood without a great deal of difficulty. With the slightest bit of progress or increased exposure her social skills are fine tuned and enhanced to best fit the socioeconomic status or standing that she aspires to.

The upbringing or family life of the black female is a significant contributing factor in how she will fare in life as an adult. Upbringing, however does not necessarily establish a bottom line as to how one will ultimately fare in life. As is the case in most races, a young black female from birth through the age of thirteen can be brought up or raised in many different types of home settings. The setting can range from that of a two-parent, loving socially functional family to a single parent, welfare role, drug environment home life that is abusive and destructive in any number of ways. Sadly, as of 1992, a young black female has less than a 50% chance to be raised in a two-parent household, thus increasing the likelihood that she will be raised in poverty.

Fully aware of the uncontrollable factors, that may inherit the lives of many young children, black and white, all people, must realize, understand and accept the fact that a child does not and can not choose his parents and the future that awaits him or her at birth. Not asking for sympathy for black children, but for all children in America who are born into situations that most would consider detrimental to *anyone's* well-being especially that of a child. Realizing that great percentages of black children are subjected to impoverished life standards, great numbers of white children are also raised in homes with incomes below the rates of poverty.

In 1989 statistics show that 20.8 million whites as opposed to only 9.3 million blacks, filled the ranks of those persons living below poverty levels. For the fiscal year of 1989 $18,630,604,733 was paid out to aid families with dependent children. Moreover statistics show that white children have a higher incidence of developmental, learning and emotional problems than black children. In 1988, 20.3 percent of white children in the U.S. were categorized with learning, developmental and emotional problems, compared to only 14.8 percent of black children at the ages of 6-11. At the ages of 12-17, 26.7 percent of white children were found to have learning problems, as apposed to only 19.5 percent of black children at this same age. These figures indicate the developmental, learning disabilities in children have a tendency to increase as children get older.

The problems with black children stem from the fact that they lack the guidance and support that teaches and establishes moral value, proper education, and self-esteem to promote well-being and personal excellence. Moreover black children are bombarded with messages that say they are incapable of high level achievement. Negative mass communication, i.e., television, newspaper articles, encourage black children to give in to defeat, as most communication suggests that black children will ultimately rate lower than white children, intellectually. More compassion is needed for all children who find themselves performing below average.

All children must be encouraged to consistently surpass themselves. (No doubt adults must be better educated in that an adult asked, how does one surpass one's self?) Simple, you set a goal, you reach it and set a higher goal, so on and so forth. Surpassing one's self is nothing more than personal, growth. Society must understand and strive to correct the damage caused to children who are the products of unplanned parenting, poverty and abuses that place them at unfair disadvantages in comparison to mainstream society.

Though much pain and suffering may occur during childhood and adolescent years, all young people must come to realize that they possess within themselves the strength and capabilities to overcome and surpass even the greatest of tragedies and hardship that they may suffer in their young lives. Oprah Winfrey, congratulations, is a prime example of a person who overcame a life tragedy that

occurred during the years of her life when it
should have been carefree, happy with
minimal amounts of pain, distrust and anger.
She was a victim of sexual abuse during her
adolescent years. Through hard work,
determination and an undying desire to be the
best that she could be Oprah Winfrey went on
to become one of the most successful women of
the nineties, a role model for all black females
and anyone else striving for excellence.

When one has occasion to become acquainted
with a young, black female who comes across
as misguided, frustrated and angry, if
concerned, (and we all should be) one must get
to know her and her background before
passing judgment. Prejudgment can stand to
make matters worse for an already innocent
victim of poverty and a dysfunctional family
environment. To help heal the wounds that
cripple and destroy bits and pieces of the
human race, we must all lend moral support to
those in need to aid in uncovering the true
value and self-worth of those afflicted by
inferiority complexes, low-self-esteem and a
lack of any type of value system.

To gain the trust of a black female in need of
moral support and guidance, one must come
across in a manner that is not condescending
in any way. Allowing a person who is
emotionally fragile to relax and become
comfortable with those who care, is a step in
the right direction toward healing the wounds
that cause social unrest, high unemployment
rates and violent crimes against others and
society. A basic, honest expression of concern
could be all that is necessary to turn a
negative and hopeless individual around to be
positive, productive and socially functional.

The negative characteristics of a black female's personality such as anger, frustration, and low self-esteem might begin to occur during adolescent years when she is exposed to social differences that influence the way different people relate to her or blacks in general. Negative personality traits of the black female may become significantly worse or they may be transformed into positive inner strengths, such as self-esteem, belief in one's self, and self-control, if properly channelled. Positive inner strengths contribute to the resulting differences in functional, successful black women and black females that become dysfunctional adults, that fill the rolls of unemployment, drug abusers, unfit parents, welfare and prison populations. These tragedies occur in every race and culture of people.

Some of us would like to think of those we label "failures" as accidents of nature with unexplainable negative differences, as we see them. Realizing that glitches in genes and chromosomes may account for many incurable differences in some of us, however, many of the tragedies among us are produced by negative social conditioning. We, fellow human beings, parents, friends, relatives, teachers, neighbors, and co-workers create many of the monsters that mingle among us just waiting to attack and explode. Human nature is that part in each of us that influences the way we think, the way we process our thoughts, the way we behave and the way we react to what we see, hear and feel, physically and mentally. Positive results occur when we have been properly conditioned and taught to develop and control our thoughts, actions, reactions and feelings making us socially acceptable to mainstream society. Negative results occur when we have

30

not been properly educated to control our behaviors, thoughts, actions, reactions and feelings that could prompt any one of us to commit violent acts against other human beings.

The black female, just like all others, regardless of race, creed, color, or sex, may experience the emotions of feeling happiness, sorrow, confidence, insecurity, superiority, arrogance, envy, or even prejudice. Every single person among us is capable of feeling or portraying any one of the aforementioned human characteristics in an eight hour, sometimes one-hour, span of time.

Though different, people are alike in many ways. Personality differences allow that the expression of any one or all of our feelings can prompt a different reaction from any number of different people. For this reason, we do not always understand how and why we relate and react to one another as we do. Our reactions to the actions of others are sometimes inconsistent and unique to what most of us may consider to be normal. Thus the black female is no different than anyone else in the area of human nature. There are specific, logical reasons why we may not always get the response we hope or intend to get from our actions, ideas and feelings. Some of us have a tendency to react in anger when we are not received the way we would like to be or think we should be. Taking into consideration the vastly varying degrees of our human natures, the way we act and react, we all must learn to accept the differences in our personalities while striving to reach acceptable levels of harmony in our families, in our relationships and among the different races of people that we must encounter on a day to day basis.

The black female is very much accustomed to adjusting her behavior to that of mainstream society. If it is the desire of mainstream society to better accommodate racial differences, mainstream society, whites in particular, must strive to better understand and accept blacks. Successful black females realize that flexibility is key if it is their desire is to prosper and grow. Mainstream society, must become more flexible to accommodate and welcome all human resources of talent and creativity. While flexibility does not suggest that one fully sacrifice one's values, morals, goals and beliefs, flexibility does, however, provide for the allowance of others to maintain self-confidence, self-esteem and worth as they attempt to initiate new ideas and explore new territories.

For a black female striving toward higher heights, it is not a rarity for her to focus more on personality or racial differences as opposed to dealing with the details of an attempted task at hand. For black females determined to reach the goals they set, it is imperative that they deal with racial hostilities and prejudice attitudes in ways that are diplomatic and non-threatening to parties that may be harmful to a black person's self-esteem and self-confidence.

Continuing to slow and hinder the advancement of all mankind, racism has been effective in stifling the growth of blacks with fragile levels of self-esteem, self-confidence and self-worth. Many blacks *accept* a second-class citizenship, thus oppressing their own progress and growth. From a personal experience, I attended the same business school with a black female friend, both of us from similar family and educational backgrounds. Upon graduation, I opted to apply for employment with a major corporation. My friend, frankly stated to me that I would not be hired, "they only hire white." I applied and got the position for which I had applied because I had not been brainwashed to believe that as a black woman I was unconditionally inferior and undeserving of that which I knew I was qualified and desired to have.

Blacks fall prey to self-oppression because they are not fully in tune with themselves in terms of their own strengths in self-determination, intelligence and worth. If blacks were more sensitive to the realities of human nature, they would know that most of the actions and behaviors of whites that suggest that they are far superior (too blacks), is in fact behaviors to make others *believe* that whites are superior, while knowing they are not. Whites are most often successful at "portraying" superiority because they discipline themselves to work harder at "*becoming*" superior to all others in obtaining power, owning businesses, and achieving higher levels of success. If blacks want to reduce their inferiority complexes and statuses they must "work" to increase their productivity to increase the output or result of their energies and actions, thereby increasing black business ownership, higher educational achievements and greater economic power which they should create and maintain with blacks, for blacks for the betterment of all mankind.

With more focus on the actions and reactions of the black female in American society that can have either negative or positive effects on the progress, growth and survival of a black female, she must set her mind to grasp everything and anything that will serve to boost her moral and motivation to go forward

33

and upward toward excellence. Of course, a black female with a light-hearted, up-beat, enthusiastic personality can receive different reactions to her positive-type personality for many different reasons as she attempts to assimilate and blend into mainstream society. The same scenario can apply to almost any situation, even where all parties are of the black race. In one instance, a black female may cause one person to react to her in a manner that is responsively, happy, welcome and cordial. In another instance, she may prompt a response that may be envious, condescending, apprehensive, aloof or rude—all negative responses to positive behavior.

Depending on the personal security of the black female, she may overlook unwarranted or unjustified negative behavioral reaction to her positive behavior...for a time or two. Repeated, negative responses may cause her to adjust her own behavior to that of being aloof, cautious and apprehensive in her own dealings with certain individuals and situations. In the worse case, negative behavior toward a black female, which she is unable to identify the cause, may prompt the black female to doubt her own self-esteem and confidence. Causing irreparable damage, she may never come to realize that most negative responses to her positive-type behavior should not be taken personally.

For the black female, open to candid and frank communication or determining what is real from what is not, the opportunity to discuss one's feelings about questionable circumstances and situations is always available if done in a way that is non-threatening or destructive to the opportunity to know the truth, about racism or discrimination, for example. Most well-

balanced, black females with socially
acceptable attitudes, will come to realize that
most perceptionally, unwarranted behavior
from others is a result of personal insecurity,
self-hatred, envy, racist, or uneducated
behavior on that persons part.

Socially, unexperienced, black females, never
realize that much of the negative treatment
that they may encounter, in life may have
nothing to do with them as an individuals. It is
very difficult for young black females to
conceive and accept that negative treatment is
often *intended* to make blacks, in general, feel
less confident and valuable as human beings
by persons who are themselves, insecure,
angry, frustrated and unsure of their own self-
worth and security of their standing in any
given situation.

The confusion, insecurity or caution that a
black female may exhibit is usually a display of
uncertainty in determining possible motives
behind the negative behavior of others. Thus
she may constantly find herself in a state of
adjustment to others until she discovers and
establishes her own sense of self, confidence,
values, goals, importance, purpose and
aspirations. Though black females realize that
racism and prejudice is a part of everyday life
for most blacks, she comes to realize that
effectively understanding and coping with the
obstacles, trials and tribulations of being black
comes with maturity and experience as one
continues with a natural, upward progression
through life.

When the black female finally establishes a
healthy attitude about her own personal value
as a person, she finds that her self-confidence
may also pose a problem. In that some people
are unsure of themselves, these are people who

have problems with people who possess and show self-confidence. Self-assured, confident black females may be viewed as arrogant, aggressive to non-blacks. The self-assured, confident black female may come across as cold, uncontrollable and disrespectful to black males with fragile egos and low self-esteem. Thus, smart, ambitious black females realize that achieving a comfort zone and level of success as a black female will not be easy, but with finesse, diplomacy, intelligence, determination and a strong will to succeed and survive in a male and white dominated society, she can and will prevail.

A mystery to most and misunderstood by others, society is responsible for the many different characteristics that the black female is forced to display in every day life in an effort to assimilate, survive and grow. For the black female, having a sense of variety within her personality is an essential tool and skill used to progress in America. Unlike the black female, black males have shown to be less likely to adapt to compromise and flexibility, thus explaining their inability to assimilate and mainstream into the societies of which they are supposed to be a part. From most aspects of the black female's efforts to survive and prosper she realizes at an early age that personal growth and stability will not be an easy task or accomplishment as she struggles among whites, black males, and other black females.

For the black female, life is a perpetual obstacle course, especially if she has set her own agenda regarding what standard of living she chooses for herself and how she feels she must function to satisfy that agenda. With all things considered, whites, black males and other black females, the ambitious, goal oriented black female, with a developed sense of awareness, sets her own sights, realizing that she must rely on her own personal instincts, experience and wisdom for survival and guidance. The black female in America, realizes she is basically on her own to achieve and accomplish a satisfying standard of living. The black female in America becomes even more alienated and isolated should she decide to go beyond the boundaries middle-class living standards or break from a heavily poverty stricken past.

The black female has been forced into independence and self-sufficiency because the black male in America cannot be relied upon to provide black females with satisfying lifestyles. Unlike white men, who support, respect, lead, protect and remain loyal to their counterpart--the white female, black males, in general, fall far short of what manhood is all about and what it was intended to be. Not only do black males show deficiencies where black females are concerned, black males also fall short in support of the black children that they father. Black males also fall short in support of one another, and the black race as a whole, thus black males are the primary cause of perpetual black oppression.

Nevertheless, the black female, attempts to remain supportive of the black male because she cannot ignore nor forget the common bond between them that they are both black Americans, descended from African ancestors, many, many years ago, who slaved together, fought together, and died together for the freedom, liberty and justice that black males of the nineties, individually take for granted. Sadly, many black females realize that if she is to survive, it is primarily on her own strength, her own will and determination that she must

depend; only to be told later in life, by black
males that she is too strong and independent
for his *"taste"* in women.

The black female, cannot help but feel
confused and frustrated as she comes to the
realization that much of the way she must
function in society can be closely related to
game playing--where almost everyone wants to
win, be first, or be on top, while the wise black
female knows that everyone cannot hold the
same winning positions simultaneously.
Likening "life" to a game, the black female
comes to notice that a great number of the
players will do almost anything to achieve
winning statuses. Confusion for the black
female sets in when others, particularly black
males, succeed in making her feel guilty about
wanting to win, wanting what most healthy,
normal human beings want and deserve out of
life--successful living.

Realizing that most people do want to win, the
black female also realizes that much of what
she desires to attain in life will involve, most
often, high-level competition, be it in the
classroom, workplace, politics or relationships.
Because competition is often fierce and rapidly
increasing, changes in the rules and
regulations become inevitable. Changes in the
way people are forced to compete against one
another is also greatly influenced by changes
in technology, economics, and most
significantly those in control, holding most of
the power.

The smart, black woman realizes that she must
seek to recognize, the ways and means of
social change. Recognizing how and why
society changes as it does, such knowledge
allows the black woman to "adapt" to the
natural flow of upward mobility and personal

growth. The astute black female being very much aware of the world around her cannot help but recognize many of the tactics used by those around her in all out efforts to win or to keep others from winning. The latter, being a strong deterrent against success, some people simply 'become" success blockers. Listed below are a few of the "types" of people in mainstream society who attempt to stand between others and success. Black females can least effort to associate with these types people. (*People types found in "Million Dollar Habits" by Robert J. Ringer.*) I would suggest that all people read this book, in our supposed efforts eliminate problems and re-establish "The American Dream."

1. <u>Drain People</u>-*People who drain you of time, energy, peace of mind, relaxation, comfort, money and whatever you possess of any value. Stay away from them.*

2. <u>Burr People</u>- *People who are irritated by those who are positive, enthusiastic and happy. Stay away from them.*

3. <u>Changers</u>-*People who want to change you. Unhappy, unless they can convert you to act, think and do as they do.*

4. <u>The Chiseler</u>-*Always has to get the best deal, the largest cut or extra bonus.*

5. <u>Conditional People</u>-*Those who willingly give gifts, with an equally, priced "string" attached.*

6. <u>Deal Gabbers</u>-*People who immediately become enthusiastic about relationships, partnerships, or business proposi- tions, only to 'always" leave you--- hanging.*

7. <u>Desperate People</u>-*Decisions and actions made by people who have nothing to lose-don't follow them.*

8. <u>Destroyers</u>-*Miserable, unhappy, negative, people, whose main objective in life is to*

destroy the confidence, enthusiasm and drive of others. Definitely stay away from these type people.

9. _Hallucinators_-People who do not acknowledge nor admit to the differences between reality, dreams and imagination.

10. _Liars_-Stay away from people who cannot and do not demonstrate their honesty.

11. Try This People-People who encourage you to try or involve yourself in illegal or unacceptable activities that you _feel_ may be detrimental to your health, well-being, reputation, safety or life--drugs for instance.

WHEN IN DOUBT--DEFINITELY--DON'T!

When black women show signs of being aware of individuals with negative intentions, black males quickly label them uncontrollable and out of control. When black females expose racism and discrimination, whites initially want to claim that claims of racism are imaginary. Smart black females adamantly realize that they must look out for their own best interests. Thus, black males resort to complaints about their inabilities to control the actions, behavior, and thinking of intelligent black females.

Quick to complain about their lack of control over black females, black males fail to gain control over the things that would grant them full manhood. Black males have very little control over their own lives, their tempers, their job security, their economic statuses and their drug problems. Blacks males should be controlling their inability to establish and maintain profitable "legal" businesses like banks, grocery stores hotels and mortgage companies. Black males should also be controlling their inability to reduce the black,

inmate jail population, their inability to
eliminate their urges to kill other black males,
their inability to set and reach goals, their
inability to control the black children that
they father.

And one of the biggest problems of all black
males should be striving to control their
inability to control their sexuality, as it (black
male sexuality) controls the every thought and
action of too many black males in America.
Regarding the black male's lack of control and
power, the black woman should be slapping
him rather than the other way around as
Shahrazad Ali suggested in her book "The
Blackman's Guide to Understanding the
Blackwoman" as a solution to the
uncontrollable, disrespectful ways of the black
woman. (But of course there is absolutely NO
need for physical violence to be inflicted on
anyone for any reason whatsoever.)

Contrary to what great masses of black males
are able to realize, black females realize that
as society "in America" changes, opportunities
for all (regardless of race and sex) increase
for improved lifestyles and standards. As a
result, to the dismay of black males in general,
the pleasure and luxuries in life become more
and more attractive to black females. On the
other hand, her counterpart-the black male- is
more likely to brood about what he does not
have, and what someone is unwilling to "give"
him, as he settles within or beneath his
already established standard of living. A great
majority of black males easily give in to defeat,
unless a circumstance involves an
unorganized, recreational sport, violent crime
or an easily obtained sexual encounter. Black
males must strive and work to change the
negative reputations that they have created
and maintained for themselves, otherwise they

41

will continue to commit the slow suicide of the entire black race, of which blacks like to label genocide.

Usually on their own, without the support of their counterparts--black males, black females, often make the decision to enhance their resources, finances, intelligence, awareness, flexibility, strength, goals, and aspirations. As inflation dictates, black females know that they must consistently increase their assets, income, wisdom, experience and intelligence to remain consistently and increasingly successful even within their own socioeconomic class or level. Equally important, ambitious black females also realize that they must increase or enhance their level of effort, discipline, awareness, productivity and enthusiasm in order to reap greater rewards from energies spent. As black females increases their strength, productivity and enthusiasm, the dissention and tension between them and black males increases, almost simultaneously. Ignored by society and sometimes black females, black males grow in frustration, never realizing what they must do to achieve the level of respect and power they desire and deserve to feel confident and sure of themselves as "men".

The problem with most struggling young black males who have reached the "age" and "physical appearance" of manhood is that they are not aware of what it means to be a "man." Certainly they want the respect and admiration due any "man." But when it comes to the responsibilities of a "man", problem-ridden black males show very little difference between males and females barring anatomy and the excessive trouble that they cause themselves. Confused, frustrated, angry and energetic, black males struggling to become

42

men, easily become resentful of black females
who understand themselves, and obviously
have a pretty good understanding of what life
is all about.

Lost in the maze of fun, games, frolic and black
male peer pressure to have even more fun,
black males become more resentful of
productive, black females striving for success,
labeling them materialistic, arrogant, selfish,
con artists, conniving, manipulative,
disrespectful and out of control. Black males
claim a total lack of comprehension as to why
black females feel they must have personal
goals and aspirations. Finding much difficulty
in mainstreaming, black males, also point to
ambition as another barrier that stands
between themselves and black females. Thus,
it becomes easy for black males to blame the
strong, independent, black "working" woman
for the breakdown of the black family
structure and many of the other ills that
plague the black race. Black males, obviously
do not realize that the black race would have
died by now if black women refused to educate,
feed, cloth, transport and provide shelter for
themselves, black children AND black males.

In striving for success or even basic survival,
black females have come to feel victimized as a
result of their achievements. Successful, or
potentially so, black women of the nineties
feel confused, frustrated, angry and sometimes
guilty for 'arious reasons. Though black
women may enjoy their newfound sense of self,
success and social position, many black females
suffer a slight sense of disillusion as a result
of the one most significant "drawback" that
attaches itself to the success of many black
women. After crossing many personal barriers
and social obstacles, far too many ambitious,
accomplished and successful black women

43

realize that self-sufficiency, self-awareness, social-awareness, and economic stability has cost them the love and understanding of their counterpart--the black man.

Among, themselves, (black women) ask themselves and each other, "was the price too high." Black women wonder do the benefits of self-fulfillment, growth, economic stability and success out-weigh the benefits of a counterpart who is supportive, loving and in tune with himself, his mate and environment? Some would say yes and some would say no. But most will agree that the choice does not exist for most black women, because her counterpart-the average black male of the nineties is unwilling to *be* supportive, loving, in tune with himself, his mate and his environment. However, most black women seriously ponder what they can do to bridge the gap between themselves, struggling black males and society without "carrying" them through life, as if they were helpless, fragile children, crying and waiting for the next feeding.

Forging ahead, the black woman has a tenacious desire and fortitude to survive and grow in a society where she is usually a minority, particularly in the workplace. A fact that has prevailed down through history, black women consistently and naturally grow in strength and wisdom, as they adapt to whatever adversities they encounter. Much like black woman of historical periods, success-minded black women of the nineties continue to do whatever is necessary to rank among the winners in life rather than those who settle into failure and defeat. Adding to the resentment that the black male already inwardly feels toward self-reliant and sufficient black women, black males also show signs of intimidation or nervousness during encounters with outwardly, (but not overly), confident black women. In my own dealings in the workplace, at racially mixed social gatherings, health spas or just out shopping, black males show obvious and prevalent signs of their "fear" of black women.

On many occasions, I have observed black males, alone in a public space with black women, who remain completely silent, for 30 minutes or more, appearing either snobbish, intimidated, or simply stupid. Upon encountering white women, regardless of how they look, pretty, ugly, fat, thin, classy or trashy, black males seem to have no problem conversing for hours on end. For what it is worth, I would surmise that these black males who find it impossible to converse with unacquainted black women but eagerly and unconditionally communicate with unacquainted white women realize that the expectation level is low if existent at all.

No doubt, black males are smart enough to realize that in encountering black women there is a level of expectation, in that black males, as a whole are deficient in their social standing as men. And no doubt, black women are perpetually on the alert to determine if she has encountered a "brother' who is further hindering or helping the cause of the black race, as they both know the black race is in desperate need of an instant and fast cure. Whereas, when a black male encounters a white woman, he first of all is quick to show the "honor" that he feels, as he has been granted his first or yet, another opportunity to shine for "a white woman." Secondly, he must realize that the level of expectation is low, if existent at all in that what ever a black male of the nineties, displays, says or exhibits is a cut above what is expected of a black male who is a member of a race of people once victimized by institutionalized slavery or servitude. At these moments, black males can feel "quite proud"-- feeling and thinking they have finally arrived. Until of course, they go to the grocery store,the malls, the workplace, the mortgage company, the bank, a restaurant, and a car wash to find that all is usually owned by men with one difference--they are white men who work harder and smarter, together, to earn the power, respect, pleasure and thrill of full manhood in *ALL* of its glory.

Instead of recognizing the black woman for the strides that she had made and continues to make against obvious odds, the struggling black male pretends to be unaware of her achievements and accomplishments. If black males are for any reason forced to acknowledge the achievements of a black woman, the acknowledgement is done to minimize the significance or importance. In the worse cases, the struggling, frustrated and envious black male sets out to "break down,", "put in place" or "bring down a notch or two" ambitious black women, striving toward success, excellence or even isolated accomplishments. To make matters worse, the insecure black male makes himself almost impossible to work with in any type of team effort to further enhance their growth as a team and as individuals.

Sometimes even the "thought" of a team effort with a black male is a remote impossibility in that the fragile black male ego will not allow for team efforts, in that some black males must feel that they are the initiator, and controller of any given situation, regardless of the reality of a particular matter. Never mind the importance or benefits of the outcome, the vast

46

majority of black males have extreme
difficulty with organized productive efforts,
barring unprofessional or recreational
activity. A problem that can and should be
corrected, black males would do much to
improve upon their own life standards, those
of the black race and the entire human race if
they could come to grips with their own
strengths and weaknesses to be channeled into
positive, productive efforts and outcomes. But,
unfortunately, blacks as a whole do not want to
deal with the actual "weaknesses" of the black
race to overcome those weaknesses, to move
toward mass, positive productive "results" that
will serve to improve upon the plight of all
people, regardless of race, creed, color or sex.

Because black males have become so
complacent and lax in their status as men,
millions of black males and black females have
become almost totally ineffective in their
communication with one another. Causing the
black race to become more and more
insignificant, half is looking up and the other
half is looking down, ready to give up, lay
down and die in willful defeat. The vast
majority of black males and females seem
incapable of relating to one another on issues
of significance or importance. More and more,
the black male and female continue to go their
separate ways--widening the gaps that already
separate black males and females.
Disheartening is the fact that elements such as
ambition, positive thinking, positive
productivity, education, self-awareness, self-
esteem, understanding goals, discipline,
commitment, fortitude and a desire to work
hard is what separate the black woman from
the black male.

The black female finds the lack communication
within the black race disturbing and

troubling. The black male does not seem to care as long as he can regularly fulfill his sexual or recreational desires. The black male will either not admit that there is a problem between the two of them that needs to be solved together or he totally blames the black woman for not supporting him in his efforts to do absolutely nothing, most of the time. As a result, the black male tells the black woman, in an arrogance tone of voice to solve the problem herself, "since she feels that there is a problem." Sarcastically, he might add, "you're superwoman--with all your degrees and high-power ideas." To finish such a conversation, a frustrated, angry black male might add, "and you may return to me with the solution IF you so desire, and I MIGHT listen." Herein, the black woman is left to feel, lonely, frustrated, sad, guilty, confused and angry. Deep inside, it is is not a rarity for an ambitious black woman to accept all blame for the lack of communication, love and understanding (and all other problems) between herself and the black male that she has chosen to love.

Or that same, positive thinking, growth and success minded black woman may come to realize that she is not totally to blame for the laziness, low-self-esteem, anger and frustration that overwhelms a vast majority of black males. She knows she cannot accept the blame for the internal problems that black males feel inside that blind them from the courage and strength they need to succeed and flourish. As mature adults, black women know that the black males that they love are unreasonable and uncompromising in their efforts to explain away their shortcomings and deficiencies as men. The black woman also knows that the display of arrogance and refusal to work with her in solving the problems of relationships and those of the struggling black male is a cover-up and disguise.

The black woman knows that the pride and ego of the troubled black male forces him to hide the anger, disappointment and frustration he feels as a result of his own personal shortcomings and lack of self-awareness. The black woman knows that black males feel cheated, defeated, socially "left out" and "shortchanged." Even social scientists are becoming aware of the fact that black males are not honestly facing their problems head on to find solutions. More and more of society, with the exception of the black male himself is coming to realize that black male arrogance is really a symbol of the hurt, pain and frustration of a male, wishing, hoping and even risking death to one day be know as a "man."

Dr. Richard Majors, a psychologist at the University of Wisconsin at Eau Clair, wrote of the black men's 'cool pose' as "empowering." Majors wrote that *through the black male's "cool pose," he can appear competent and in control of adversity.* As a black woman, I would have to agree that black males *do* adopt "mannerisms" or "attitudes" as sources of dignity and worth to mask the sting of their failures and frustrations. I know that the failures and frustrations that black males hide behind arrogant gestures and attitudes could easily be transformed into positive-mental attitudes, if black males could at least allow themselves to see themselves as they really are. If black males want to change for the better, they must embrace the courage to confront their personal weaknesses and social shortcomings head on and face forward.

49

Black women are not impressed by black male arrogance because they know that one in four black males, aged 20 to 29 is in prison, on probation or on parole--more than the total number of black men in college. Black women also know that the unemployment rate for black males is more than twice that for whites. And black women are also aware that the leading cause of death among black youth is homicide--that 48 percent of black males between 15 and 19 who died were shot (with whites males at only 18 percent). Moreover, black women cannot ignore the fact that black males in Harlem can expect to live less years that men in Bangladesh and that nationally, black males aged 15 to 29 die at a higher rate than any other age group except 85 year-olders. For these reasons, black women are very sad and emotionally pained by the suffering of the black male that he, primarily, brings upon himself.

It pains the black woman even more to know that her counterpart (the black male) can not and will not admit to his weaknesses, deficiencies, shortcomings and strong need for help in defining "black" manhood. In most cases, frustrated and angry black males struggling to be seen, heard and to survive are unwilling to take even *one*, long, hard look at themselves to honestly see their strengths and their weaknesses, especially as they relate to mainstream society. The black males who have recently fallen through social cracks or will soon fall are almost encouraged by society, their friends and their families to fail as most of society so willingly accepts the negative-producing thoughts and actions that black males almost force upon others with their arrogant and often-time scare tactical mannerisms and gestures.

Black males thinking that they have been accepted, have only been dismissed as hopeless, as others shake their heads in pity as they give up on black males who willfully propel themselves toward, defeat, destruction and early deaths. Though black males appear strong, the strength that a vast majority of them portray is actually the strongest barrier between them and the help that they need from others to point them in the 'direction" "toward" the pathways of survival and success. Black males, whether they want to admit it or not need help in sorting out their frustrations, strengths and weaknesses.

As a pointer, I would suggest that all blacks (beginning at the age of age 10) buy and read every single word in my book "A Black Woman Speaks" to make them aware of what needs to be changed to end the destruction of the black race. When reading, "A Black Woman Speaks," I also suggest that the reader begin with a bright, high visible marker, highlighting all pertinent points. The reader should also highlight all statements or passages that they do not understand or agree with. These passages should be used in discussion with family, friends, and all other associates to raise the conscious level of blacks and the rest of society.

With a great many acquaintances, I am aware that thousands of people, black, white and all other races in between (from the ages of ten through 60, degreed and non-degreed) read at levels far below what they should be. I strongly suggest that people with deficient reading abilities stop lying to themselves and others and read (and understand) every single word in "A Black Woman Speaks" if it takes an entire year. As friends and family, we should challenge one another's ability to read and comprehend the written word to end oppression, poverty, illiteracy, violence, unemployment, disease, drug abuse, child abuse and the decline of well-being for the human race around the world. I was even a little disappointed in the "presentation" of Anita Hill during a Detroit appearance/talk in 1992. (The Law Professor in the Clarence Thomas Hearings regarding sexual harassment.)

Secondly, I would suggest that all blacks read *"The psychology of Winning, by Dr. Denis Waitley* to help blacks develop the winning attitudes they need to survive, prosper and grow. Dr. Denis Waitley, lists ten qualities of a total winner. They are:

1. *Positive Self-Awareness: I understand where I am coming from.*
2. *Positive Self-Esteem: I like myself (honestly)*
3. *Positive Self-Control: I make it happen for me.*
4. *Positive Self-Motivation: I want to, I can.*
5. *Positive Self-Expectancy: Good, better, perfect.*
6. *Positive Self-Image: I see me changing, growing.*
7. *Positive Self-Direction: I have a game plan.*
8. *Positive Self-Discipline: Place a bet on yourself to succeed.*
9. *Positive Self-Dimension: There is harmony between me and my environment.*
10. *Positive Self-Projection: Project the above nine qualities.*

Of course, I realize that are a great number of black males who are striving, growing and reaching for success. And yes, the black race is, no doubt, proud of the Michael Jacksons, the

Michael Jordans, the Bill Cosbys, black teachers, black administrators, black doctors, black lawyers and black business owners. However, there are far too many black males who are being "snuffed out" everyday by the ravages of unemployment, drug abuse, violence, illiteracy, and negative attitudes...black males who will never live to present their true talents and worth, black males who will never experience manhood.

And I realize that a lot of black males will take a defensive attitude toward the information in this book, asking whether or not I am implying that black females have not fallen through social cracks, left their children, abused drugs, dropped out of school and chosen welfare over gainful employment? Absolutely not, because black females also have some very serious problems, that they too have caused for themselves and the black race. Just as in all races, there have always been some people who will require more education, support, guidance and motivation to reach their potential as successful human beings. But, I do believe if all black males were properly guided toward the ranks of full manhood, (as proud black men) most problems of the black race would be solved. If all black males/men had their acts together, black females/women would have very little choice but to be supportive, committed, intelligent, disciplined and hard working women for the betterment of the black race as well as that of the human race. All black males should be raised to collectively maintain satisfying living standards for the entire black race, along with the aid of the black woman.

Black females, are in large part, responsible for the state of poverty that they subject their children to. Many young black women of the

53

nineties are aware that they involve themselves with black males who are jobless, drug addicts, criminals or just plain irresponsible and immature. Yet black females still choose to have far greater instances of out-of-wedlock childbirths than white females. Sadly and pathetically, the percentage of black females who gave birth to children (ages 15-44) in the year ending June 1990 was 56.7 percent. The percentage for white females was only 17.2%. In my opinion, this problem is one of the most impacting tragedies that black females subject upon themselves, the black race and most harmfully upon the lives of innocent, black children. Black females must consider the children *before* getting pregnant. And with all the available education, there is no intelligent reason for unwanted pregnancies, barring rape.

So even with all the problems of the black female, how did she escape the mass affliction of self-destruction and oppression that has hit black males in practically every community, city and state across America? What motivated the black female to choose the pathways of self-awareness, positive productivity and success oriented attitudes and action...as opposed to those of defeat, self-destruction and death? Why does the black female sometimes seem to have an unending supply of drive and determination--even against immense odds and obstacles? Why is the black woman so concerned about growth and progress while most of her counterparts--black males are not?

The successful, black woman, in many ways and cases, has the black male to thank for her success and strength. As a black woman, I can personally identify and relate to the broken bond between black males and females. Increasing since the seventies, black males

have chosen to go their own way [ALONE] to
discover themselves and life, leaving the black
female, [with no choice] but to also discover
herself and life.   Going their separate ways,
black males take and continue to take wrong
turns, beginning as early as the ages of
sixteen or seventeen sometimes younger...down
dead-end roads to self-inflicted social and
physical destruction or death.   Black males,
take turns and choose pathways   that   in 1992
still lead them toward violence, drugs,
destruction and death.

Though some survive while rendering
themselves socially crippled, maimed, tired,
frustrated and angry, young black males
obviously make choices that greatly differ
from black females, who too are black
Americans, descendants of African ancestors,
sailed from Africa, dealing with the same
problems that prey on the black male.   Failing
to understand how so many black females of
the nineties could be fairing so much better,
than black males of the nineties, some black
males act as though, he and his counterpart--
the black females have come from two TOTALLY
different worlds.

By successful and struggling black males alike,
a good number of accomplished or successful
black women are viewed or labeled by black
males as "uncontrolled" or in need of being
"tamed" by marriage.   Black unmarried women
do desire to be married but not for the reason
of being owned, controlled or tamed.   Wrestling
with their confidence and sympathy-prompted,
guilt, black women are made to feel ashamed of
success and ambition by black male
counterparts who may not be fairing quite as
well or as well as they think they should be.

"Insecurity" is oftentimes a significant part of the black female character because on the one hand she is forced to be strong in support of herself only to find herself unacceptable to the black male because of her strength. (On an Oprah Winfrey Show on Thursday, July 23, 1992 I was shocked to see that white women also suffer from the fact that their mates appreciate but hate at the same time, "female" personal strength) Some black men, sympathetic to the plight of black women liken the 'syndrome" of the internal fight between strength and weakness to that of "tight-rope walking." A black male friend stated that "women really do have it hard in dealing with black males "today." "They must constantly be on their toes," adding, "one strong move in any direction, can destroy a relationship. As black women struggle to fend for themselves toward comfortable standards of living, they must deal with black male egos that are much to fragile to cope with the strength of strong, ambitious, black women, determined to survive.

Black males, with fragile egos, complain that the black woman does not *need* him, especially if the black woman presents herself as a "thinking" person. With hurt feelings, black males seem unable to realize and/or accept that the intelligence and strength of the black female should be looked upon as a valuable asset. Providing an example of the frustrated, black male thought process, black males often feel that, "the strength and intelligence of the black woman is another weapon, used by "the white man" to destroy him.

Though, hard for black males to understand, the black woman's rejection of absolute "control" over the use of her natural and learned capabilities is the black woman's attempt to help black males recognize, understand and appreciate the beauty and benefits of her value as a strong, intelligent, person, destined to succeed in life. Observing everyday life, within the black race, many black women have come close to destruction—physically and or mentally at the hands of black males with whom black females attempt to function, work, live and love. I cried so hard and deeply as I watched the Detroit, 11:00 p.m. news on July 22, 1992 as the face of a young, beautiful, vibrant, young, black girl of 17 flashed across the screen. She had been chased out of her own home and shot to death by her black, male boyfriend. Just days before she had asked her mother for a gun for protection from the boyfriend who, days later took her life; her mother said, NO. "Guns are not the way to handle things." Police had previously been called to inform them about the danger that the boyfriend posed to the young, black female. The police requested that *she* "stay away from him." Days later, into her home he barged, chasing her, gunning her down, to take away, her young and precious life of only 17 years.

Before her untimely death, the young girl told her mother that "she would be somebody, someday." Business school was the plan of the young girl, killed by the black male who shared the love of a girl, only seventeen. The pain that I felt was as intense of if she had been my sister or daughter. How, I asked myself, could a black male, take the life of a black female, whom he probably loved. Hopefully the day will come when black males will have erased and eliminated the anger and pain that make them erupt in blind, violent rages to destroy themselves and the black females that they are supposed to love.

It seems that the black male is unaware, that even through the black female's strength, the black female is very fragile, very soft and loving. The black female is in need of black males who are able to become strong, educated, hard-working, supporting and self-controlled, successful and loving black men. If the black male is to fully regain the black female's trust, the black female seeks and needs to feel confident that the black male can appreciate and accept her qualities without envious resentment, allowing her to flourish and bloom for the benefit of him, the black race and all of man and womankind.

Trying hard to be strong, but not too strong, (for the sake of the black male ego) some black females deal with the "tight rope syndrome" almost on a daily basis in life as well as in love. Having to function within the contradiction, between the strength and courage to survive and false weakness for the sake of love, black females can not relax nor fully express themselves in relationships with frustrated black males with large egos, as fragile as the most priceless of crystal. In the absence of the black male, the black female is forced to be strong and deliberate to uphold the ends and sides of the black race, where black males have left their positions as men for the sake of recreation, defeat or death. In his presence, the black female is expected to be passive, carefree and honored that he is present, though lacking in any type of meaningful purpose One male friend suggested, "if you want to impress and win a black guy over, "don't talk." "Don't reveal "any" of your intelligence and inner-strength to him." I tried it, it worked to get the guy, but I felt as human as a blank sheet of paper. It did not work for me.

Black women hiding and stifling their intelligence and strength pose dangerous and serious problems for the entire black race as well as for individuals directly involved with them. As blacks are most oppressed when compared to other races in almost all areas of life, blacks cannot afford to destroy and throw away valuable resources found in the areas of strength, intelligence, determination and wills to succeed. Hiding strength and faking stupidity erect additional, unnecessary barriers between the black male and female, in that they are unable to face the realities of who they are as individuals relative to suffering, poverty, depravation and oppression. Until the black male and female can somehow learn to recognize, accept, enhance, nurture and present the value in one another, they will continue to be ineffective in dealing with issues and problems that plague the black race.

Solutions to the problems that separate and alienate the black female from the black male can only come from their mutual cooperation, effort and desire to come together in an effort to reverse the overall downward trend of the black race. Together, the black male and female, on all levels must *work* to solve the problems that plague, primarily the black race as well as society such as high unemployment rates, crime, drug abuse, illiteracy and poverty. For the black male, the black female and the entire human race, it is important that they solve the problems of their relationships so that the unnecessary pain and suffering of oppression can end forever. Together, black men and women can go on to maximize the potential of all blacks in America to contribute to the healing of the black race, the human race and the world in which we all must live.

59

It is a very strong desire in some black women to use their strength, knowledge hopes and dreams to solve the problems that prey upon the black race and society at large. Fully aware that the problems that exist between the black female and male did not formulate in one day or one year, it is not expected that the problems will simply "disappear" overnight. But, from a foundation of quiet, unselfish, understanding, open communication, determination and hard work, one of the most significant problems within the black race (the separation of the black male and black female) can be alleviated. Solving the problem of separation and alienation between black males and females, black mothers and fathers and black children, can lead to a unity among the black race that can stand to help restore, the structure of the black family and great American dreams, which may one day lead to the peace and prosperity on earth that most of us only dream, talk, sing and read about.

Starting at the root of what ails the black race, it is absolutely necessary to realize and accept the fact that if the black female has a problem, the black male has a problem that inevitably trickles within and throughout all of society negatively effecting the livelihood, prosperity, safety, health, security, happiness and future of every single human being on the face of the earth in America and every single other country known to mankind. The black woman is often made to feel that she must personally shoulder the blame for the breakdown of the family structure--which has led to many other problems that exist within the black race.
Is this to say that she (the black woman) has been the leader, the strength and the very "backbone" of the entire black race? Some blacks would say "yes." Where the blame for

the problems of the black race must lie is unimportant. It *is* important, however, that blacks of all ages, male and female accept responsibility for the plight of the black race and collectively commit to correct the problems. Before a commitment can be made among the members of the black race, the black woman must first of all convince the black male that they "together" must take responsibility the current plight of the black race. The black male and female must stop blaming "the system," "society" or "the white man" (as they say) for unemployed blacks, blacks in prison, drug addicted blacks, unwed black mothers and the rampant death of black males, killed by other black males, when not a single white person is anywhere in sight. All blacks must stop the finger pointing and judgment of one another and aggressively WORK to end poverty, illiteracy, violence, drug abuse and the suicide of the black race.

No doubt, white racist messages and actions have been successful in convincing some blacks that they are inferior with inferior intellects that render them completely incapable of functioning and succeeding in mainstream society. Masses of blacks have actually come to believe that if the plight of blacks in America is to change and improve for the better, change will occur as a result of the initiative, establishment and maintenance of white society to initiate those changes. I say this is a fantasy that will "never" become reality. As we are all supposed to be created equal, no real man and real woman could actually believe and "wait" for outside sources to improve upon the quality of life of which one has complete control.

Though a vast majority of twentieth century blacks are far removed from the degradations of slavery, the mentality seems to have been inherited. Losers, wait and "expect" to feel the pain and suffering of oppression, discrimination and racism from themselves and others--thus they do, until the day they die. Winners think, act, learn and work to "create" the "opportunities" that will grant them peace, prosperity, equality, happiness and success throughout their entire lives. Black have to trade their negative, poor attitudes for attitudes rich in success, peace, happiness and the drive to bring about the positive changes they seek.

As a black woman, I can say that the black woman is strong in many ways, as she has been throughout history. Black females have always willingly and effectively accepted problem solving leadership roles whenever opportunities present themselves. Black women have been *forced* to function as the leader and strength of certain structures, (specifically the black family structure) after the departure of her counterpart, the black male. White women struggled to be equally accepted into the workforce during 1848-1920. Slavery, going back as far as 1444 had already made "work" a natural way of life for black women in America, though wrong it was. Establishing a pattern, black women were forced to struggle and survive on their own as black marriages were not considered legal entities during slavery, thus a black man and woman could be separated at the will under the authority of their "owners."

Slavery, abolished for many years, black males of the nineties have the ability to set the standards by which their families should live and function. Separated only by divorce, desertion or death, some black men see to it that the families they create live happy,

prosperous and successful lives.   Fortunately
there are thousands of black men who set and
maintain high standards as husbands and
fathers to the black women and children of the
family structures that they create.   Black
children need to be raised to reverse the
ravages of poverty, broken homes and self-
inflicted black oppression.

Though some black males may remain
"connected" to their families as husbands and
fathers, some black males have difficulty
acting as authoritative figures, decision
makers or leaders of the household and family.
The black woman with traditional values
cannot help but wonder is her mate, "the black
male" really the superior one as society
suggests?   The black woman wonders, is he, the
black male, really the stronger of the two
sexes, barring brawn?   Is he, the black male,
comfortable as the backbone of the family--
even with the support that the modern day
black woman is capable of providing?   Deep
inside, the black woman yearns to reach the
manhood of the black male lost in his own
frustration, anger and confusion.   Black males
must reach out and accept the assistance of the
black woman, if they are to ever see true
manhood.

Judging from the plight of the black family
and the black race, the black male has become
too laid back to care whether or not he reaches
manhood.   Too many black males are lazy,
passive and complacent because they no longer
have to fight, like their forefathers for the
basic rights of manhood--to stay with the
family, to be paid for an honest day's work, to
provide love and support to the black family.
In the nineties, the black woman, watches as
he (the black male) willingly walks away from

all that was once treasured and sacred--the
black woman and black children.

The black woman of the nineties wonders, how
did it all begin--the separation of the
twentieth century black male and female. I
must look back to when it began--not back to
the days of slavery when the black man had no
choice in leaving his wife and children, as he
was "sold" away, but back to the days when he
had a choice, to stay or leave by willful
separation or divorce. As of 1950, year after
year, more and more black males choose to
leave their women and children to survive
whatever way they can. The following figures
are a result of "choices" that black males make.

In 1950 17.2% of black households were headed
by women, households with no husbands, with
children under the age of 18. In 1960 the
figure increased to 24.4%; in 1970 to 34.5% in
1980; to 45.9% and in 1990 the figure reached
56.2%. In 1990 more than half of black women
with children were left to fend for themselves
against the ravages of everyday life, social
problems and tragedies.

As presented by the 110th Edition of the
Statistical Abstract of the United States the
following data shows how black children have
faired in family life as a result of the choices
that black males and females make regarding
unwed or single parenthood. In 1970, out of
nine million, four hundred twenty-two
thousand, only fifty-eight point five percent
(58.5%) of black children in America lived
with both parents; just slightly more than
half. Twenty-nine point five percent (29.5%)
lived with the mother only. Seventy point five
per cent (70.5%) of U.S. black children had to
live in fatherless homes. For white children

64

only seven point eight percent (7.8%) had to live in fatherless homes.

During the same period, two point three percent (2.3%) of black children lived with the father only. Nine point seven (9.7%) lived with neither parent. Only four point two percent (4.2%) of the fatherless homes were due to death.

Surely, the absence of black males in the black family structure has been a significant contributing factor to the strength, independence, frustration, anger and fortitude of the black woman. The black woman has been forced to become unaccustomed to working without the black male because of his voluntary absence. Even in the home, the black woman has been forced to live a dual role, one as the mother of her children and as the father of her children. With prison, crime and drug statistics as they are in the nineties, proof has been given that performing the roles of provider, mother and father has been an impossible feat for the black woman, though some have done quite well. The black woman has done the best she could in shouldering the responsibilities of two--a man and a woman.

The year 1988 continued the increasing trend of black children living family lives with no father in the home. Out of nine million, six-hundred thousand, ninety-nine children, only thirty-eight point six percent (38.6) enjoyed a family life with two parents present. This figure represents a twenty percent (20%) drop in two-parent households for black children in only eighteen (18) years. The eighties produced an even larger population than the seventies of blacks crippled by self-inflicted oppression within the black family.

Fifty-one point one percent (51.1%) of black children lived in homes with only the mother present while only sixteen percent (16%) of white children had to live in fatherless homes in 1988. What a startling, drastic, pathetic and sad contrast. Black males have created inequalities for their own children in the most harmful and damaging way--parental desertion. I can say pathetic because as a black woman, this problem is a part of me. Moreover, I plan to be a part of the solution that will help blacks realize and present their true excellence and value.

Almost twenty years later, as we approach the year 2000, the black woman is able to rely even LESS on her counterpart--the black male to assist her in the leadership, guidance and support of black children. The "sound" of the year, "2000" has much too beautiful a ring to it to receive the problems of the "nineteen-nineties." Thus "we" have seven (7) years to make a change. The black woman is both furious and saddened by the crime, drugs, unemployment and illiteracy that so many black children fall prey to. If, black males stay, as role models, father figures, leaders, teachers and friends to their children,-- "society, would be a much better place."

The inferiority complexes that afflict, restrict and consume black children begin in their own homes--their fatherless homes. Blacks, Afro-Americans, can not afford to continue to blame others for one of the most horrible crimes that we (blacks) ourselves are also guilty of--racial discrimination. How can little black boys possibly grow up to respect themselves as black men when they never experience what it feels like to respect a black man--there is no black man in most black

66

homes for little black children to respect? And
how can little black girls grow up to respect
black men when they, too, never get the
chance of giving respect to a black man? The
fathers that should mean more to black
children than life almost itself--are not in the
home. Absent black "men" from the black
home is one of the primary reasons for the
bitterness, frustration and anger of black
women, young black adults, black teenagers
and little black children.

Irresponsibility on the part of black males is
another primary reason for the lack of respect
from the black woman that black males
complain about and long for. Black women and
children should be able to look to black men to
equalize some of the injustices that they suffer
as blacks in America. Black women and
children cannot look to black males for
guidance, protection and support against the
ravages of things like poverty because black
males, collectively, do not realize that they
have the capabilities to work, to create better
life standards for themselves, their families
and that of the entire black race.

Blacks since, the days of slavery have always
been expected to fail, especially without, direct
supervision, guidance and constant prodding.
Because, society and even blacks themselves
continue to insinuate and suggest that blacks
will fail, society and blacks themselves have
very low expectation levels for blacks. BUT,
once blacks CHANGE THEIR OWN PERSONAL
EXPECTATIONS, to that of EXPECTING TO WIN OR
SUCCEED, blacks will no longer willfully,
subject themselves and each other to illiteracy,
oppression, unemployment, poverty, welfare,
drug addiction violent crime, and the overall
suicide of the black race. Black children can

67

and must look to their own black fathers, mothers, sisters, brothers, aunts, uncles, cousins, friends, associates AND THEMSELVES to right many of the wrongs that have increasingly plagued the black race.

If black mothers and fathers, as we approach the year 2000, want social equality for themselves and their children in America, blacks must STOP stripping their own sons and daughters of equality--in the home, in the classroom, and in the community? Black males and females MUST realize that EQUALITY MUST FIRST begin in the home WITH ONE THING--A FUNCTIONAL SET OF PARENTS--A MARRIAGE BETWEEN TWO STRONG, SUPPORTIVE, LOVING, UNDERSTANDING, CARING AND HARDWORKING INDIVIDUALS--A MAN AND A WOMAN WHO WANT SUCCESS FOR THEMSELVES AND THE CHILDREN THEY GIVE BIRTH TO, RAISE OR MAY ENCOUNTER ANYWHERE, ON ANY GIVEN DAY, AT ANY GIVEN TIME OF DAY.

It seems as though the vast majority of black males in America no longer value the rights that their forefathers fought and died for. The frustration, born of the black woman, is that she has not and can not forget that the black female was once protected, respect and supported by the black man-- (at least) to the VERY best of his ability within the confines of slavery and segregation. Though not often said, it is the black male who is largely responsible for the breakdown of the black family structure. It is the black male who is responsible for the increasing destruction and demise of himself--the black man. No time for anger or finding fault, it is not genocide that will end the life of the black man. It is suicide that will end the life of the black man if he does not willingly face and deal with the harsh realities of his, personally, willful destructive existence.

Born in the fifties, I can personally relate to the serious and sad circumstance that blacks have created for themselves. Late enough to slightly bypass many of the injustices of blatant and extreme racism but early enough to appreciate the trials and tribulations of the black race during the fifties and sixties. I could feel a personal appreciation for the celebration of Thurgood Marshall as he announced his retirement as a member of the U.S. Supreme Court.

A very significant victory of Thurgood Marshall's came just two years before I was born. As an attorney, Thurgood Marshall, won *Brown vs. Board of Education of Topeka*. The case, termed, a landmark, ended the legal basis for segregation in America. Knowing that black men are capable of creating successful life standards, it was a black man, Thurgood Marshall who changed the way I would function in life, as a black female, just two years before I was born...and to him I am grateful. Hence, I feel compelled to contribute something to America, the world that will one day make life easier and more comfortable for future generations. Every single, man, woman and child on the face of the earth should be raised to "give back" in appreciation for the life given to them.

Unable to emphasize enough the importance, benefits and beauty of a two-parent home, fate was kind enough to have me born and raised of a family with both parents in the home. (something I had no control over) To me and for me, the presence of a male image has made all the difference in the world affecting and shaping my attitudes, behavior and actions

69

from childhood through (functional) adulthood This is not to say that my family life was above average or privileged. As I recall, it felt socially "fair", "adequate" and equal by comparisons to my peers, extended families and television families. Ethical morals, values and growth, achieving expectations are the fibers that bind and propel families "together" toward unified and individual excellence and success.

Most neighborhood families, in the fifties, in my immediate environment had both parents in the home. I do recall several single parent, female headed households. As I saw it, during the fifties and sixties, single parent families were somewhat of a rarity. Because there were so few, I can only surmise that black men and women married at earlier ages--between eighteen and twenty-two and they stayed married.

Providing for me the stark realities that two-parent homes were *not* the prevailing norm for blacks in the sixties, on Saturday, July 25, 1992, I met a young black man of thirty-three at a local book store who told me of his tragic childhood in a fatherless home. The young man started by saying that he had five brothers and sisters, all with different fathers. He went on to tell me how his mother had sat him down at the innocent age of six, telling him that his "father" was coming to meet him. At the age of six, he was to meet his father for the very first time. He was instructed by his mother to be nice and "respectful" to the father he had never seen before, during the entire six years of his life. At the "meeting", he went on to tell me that his father, talked with him briefly and gave him "a" dollar. Continuing, his story he said, he gave the dollar back to his father as he had not been in his life and he knew he was not there to stay. With the wisdom and emotion of only six years that ONE DOLLAR could not appease a six-year old; even while imagining how much ice-cream a "whole" dollar would buy in the sixties. Listening with earnest sincerity, I had to put forth a strong and honest effort to hold back my tears, because I could see and feel the hurt that this 33-year old young black man felt as he recalled the one single memory of his "father" and "the dollar. I asked him had he seen his father since that day. He stated that he had not heard from, nor seen his father since the day of "the one dollar meeting.

I feel, as I will always will, that the two parent (male/female) family unit is a symbol of the past, present and future of mankind. "Family" was once significant and important to individuals, the various races and to society at large. During the fifties, there seemed to be an expressed or unspoken common bond between the black man and woman of togetherness, love, understanding, loyalty, strength and "better days ahead" that carried on through the seventies.

Better days, for blacks did come. Opportunities for blacks started to improve considerably in the seventies. Improvements came in the areas of economic growth, opportunities, equality, employment, social acceptance, social freedoms and education. Blacks were beginning to enjoy many of the qualities and luxuries of life that those of the "majority" enjoyed in America. BUT, as blacks begin to prosper, the children begin to suffer. Within the black race, expectations were lowered as "times" and "circumstances" became less stressful and difficult in everyday life. "Hard times" for blacks became less hard, allowing blacks to relax a little, play a little and party a lot.

With all the newfound freedoms and opportunities, the black male's need, for the black woman decreased. Fewer black males were forced to come home, tired, frustrated and worn and beaten by the ravages of segregation, unequal pay and everything else that could make life miserable for both blacks and whites before the luxuries of "convenience" "technology" and rampant "social vices" that changed the way we all live and function. The newly acquired social advantages and opportunities decreased the black male's respect and appreciation for family, loyalty, growth, and in some cases pride in himself as a MAN.

Easy access to almost every available element that life in America has to offer black males made a bee line to trouble, self-destruction and death. As life became easier for black males, long after slavery and blatant discrimination, black males adopted the attitude that the only requirement in "achieving "manhood" is that one need only be anatomically equipped. Non-black men, in more cases, have been able to hold on to the essence of their manhood, passing it within and throughout their races and generation. Male development into that of a man, requires that a male be willing and capable of securing one's own well-being and that of his wife and children. Non-black men "almost" always seem to come out ahead and above black men, yet all men are supposed to have been created equal. Black males, as a group, are too passive in areas that matter most, like family, education, racial loyalty, economic security, economic growth, socially acceptable values, social responsibility and awareness.

Contrary to what many black males believe and feel, black females/women continue to feel a natural instinct to morally support, admire, love, appreciate and respect black men...beliefs and feeling that begin with childhood. These instincts remain securely intact if the first men that they come to know--their fathers, brothers, uncles, cousins and nephews and friends function and present themselves as responsible and reliable human beings, first to themselves and then to others.

The black female has watched the black man make significant strides, of which she can be very proud...and she is. But she has also experienced a significant decline in knowing she has a counterpart--the black male that is concerned about preserving the integrity and pride of the black man particularly for his children and generations to follow.

The black male will even blame the black woman for his loss of integrity and pride. Black males often claim that it is the black woman's lack of support and interest in him that has led him astray. Ultimately black males like to blame the "independence" of the black woman for the many problems that plague the black race. The black males says that he can no longer reach the black woman. None better than the black woman realizes, that it was and still is the black male himself that is responsible for the "independence" of the black woman and his separation from her. The black male pushed and forced the black female beyond his own reach.

Increasing every year since the mid-seventies, the black male willingly decided to "put off" marriage for the future. The black male, now has "options." Consciously or subconsciously, the young black male, upon reaching adulthood, no longer needs nor seems to want the support of the black female. Beginning with the seventies, the black male has almost

73

unlimited "opportunities." The Army, the Navy, college, women, bachelorhood...total "freedom" calls his name. Determined to sample every, single spice of life that life offers--black males no longer feel compelled to choose one woman, as a wife..to feed, clothe, house, love and have his children. From the statistics, black males must tell black women, "I will give you the children, but you must handle the responsibilities...alone." Black females, must reply, "I'll take it." (A deal I will never understand.) Perhaps, not considering the consequences of their choices black males simply want to hold on to their "freedom"--have a little fun, perhaps a lot of fun. Looking back, most would never believe that "their choices" would lead them to death and destruction at the hands of violent crime, drug addiction, unemployed-poverty and death "by default." (Wrong place, wrong time.)

In the early seventies, many young black males in their early twenty's concluded that they were not quite ready for the responsibilities of a wife, a home and family. This attitude was understandable and basically acceptable because most young Americans (regardless of race) had begun to "put off" marriage until later. From statistics, it was only the black male who also decided to "put off" growing, learning working and living.

As the black male decided against "taking a wife" his counterpart, the black female was coming of age, entering, adulthood-- womanhood. Upon reaching the age of eighteen and most likely successful completion of high school, black females were facing a new dilemma. The prevailing question became "What do I do with my life? What are my choices? "My High School sweetheart does not want to get married...just yet."

74

During the seventies black women, by the thousands, chose college as a pastime...while waiting for black males to marry them. Some black females immediately got jobs, out of high school. Most were fortunate enough to recognize and take advantage of the "positive" choices that life in America offers. Black females, in the seventies, realized that they had the opportunity and the courage to go in any number of "progressive" directions. Though some may have chosen to do nothing and waste their lives, this was probably not a very popular or wise choice for twentyish-year old black females of the seventies, or any time, for that matter.

Of course, a large majority of young black women would have preferred to get married, become wives and mothers...staying in the home. Unfortunately, in many cases, the black male had taken away the option of marriage as a "trade off" for his own freedom and independent (single) lifestyle. As a result, black females established for themselves "a lifestyle" without even being aware of it. The black woman, being who and what she is, naturally flexible, became accustomed, comfortable and most importantly, good at making a way for herself. For many black, successful, women, a career was not a conscious decision or consideration...though it turned out that way.

Most likely, not many black females, chose to be free, independent and in complete control of their own lives...free, independent and in control is what black males set out to be. Very few, black females, "set out" to personally create financial security and independence for themselves. Even so, the black woman began to

75

grow, intellectually, socially and financially. Because of the "old" standard value system wherein men were the "breadwinners" and "wage earners" many women of the seventies were not immediately comfortable with their new status in life-independent and financially, comfortable. As the case remains in the nineties, black women wanted marriage, a family of her own...while great numbers of black males still choose freedom, social uncertainty, relaxation, absentee fatherhood, aimless activity, unemployment, violence, drug addiction, prison, destruction, and death.

Because marriage was not to be, for many black women, they adapted. They continued to enroll in colleges. Some got jobs, some did both, often out of boredom. Many black females had no counterparts--black males--to occupy their time and energies. Thus, black females began to assimilate into mainstream society. Hence, black women were, as they still are, consistently afforded the opportunity to enhance the education of their cultural backgrounds--common sense, moral values, ethical standards, self-esteem and racial pride. Black women discovered an abundance of new AND exciting opportunities; opportunities available to anyone in pursuit of an increased quality of living. The opportunities were, (as they remain) in a variety of areas, such as: employment, travel, civic involvement, free enterprise, entertainment, politics, communication, etc.

Opening many doors, the non-threatening, nature of the black woman serves as an asset. She possesses a natural tendency to be receptive to new opportunities, change, new ideas and challenges. Though not always willing to except the "status quo" black females are open to compromise. Compelled to

76

determine what is best and right for them, black women, with pride, dignity and determination, aggressively seek, reach, work and *EXPECT* to reach the goals that they set for themselves.

Very much aware of her social environment, the black woman does not willingly accept inequality. Though the black man has done much in acquiring social equality, for the black race, many "young" black males have become passive, content and complacent, as it was their *forefathers*, that worked, fought and died for the freedoms that most blacks enjoy today.

Black males often complain that black women are overly competitive and materialistic. Black males label the black woman's desire for a quality lifestyle as petty and trivial. The inability of black males to understand and recognize the importance of "creating" and "maintaining" economic power is yet, another reason for the frustration of black women. The black male resents the black woman's desire for a standard of living that is equal to her non-black female counterparts. Additionally black males have a tendency to resent the ambition of the black woman because, a large majority of black males are unable to step up to the challenge of upward mobility, personal growth and improved living standards.

Some black males go so far as to say that black women want to be white as a result of the endless hours spent watching soap operas and other non-black television shows that depict high standards of living. Because great numbers of black males accept sub-standard lifestyles, it is expected that black women should also accept sub-standard living

77

standards. The opposing viewpoints regarding living standards poses yet another problem between the black male and female. Frustrated and feeling defeated, strong willed, ambitious black women will usually go on to higher heights, leaving black males to wallow in their own stagnation and self-deprivation.

Adding fuel to an already smoldering fire, the black male becomes more resentful of the black woman as she seems to be more readily accepted by mainstream society. Making matters worse between the black male and black woman, the black woman is more successful in minimizing racial gaps in earning power between her counterparts than he is of his. Out of love for the black man, the black woman takes the blame for much of the anger that the black man displays when in fact he is angry and disappointed with himself.

The black male "presents" himself as strong, intelligent, self-respecting, with an even stronger sense of pride. If this is so, why is the difference between black males and his white male counterpart significantly wider than the difference between female black and white counterparts? Whatever the reason, it is black males who must desire, work and EXPECT to more equally balance the scales by which society must measure the productivity, behavior and activity of the population.

On Friday, September 20, 1991 an article appeared in the Detroit Free Press describing the unequal earnings of black males in comparison to their white male counterparts. The source was a U.S. Department of Commerce census study, in 1989-1990. The results described the salary differences based on average annual earnings of full-time workers twenty-five (25) and older. The findings were also based on education, race and sex.

Earnings with: Four Years of High School

Black Males
$20,280
Black Females
$16,440

White Males
$26,510
White Females
$16,910

Black males earned $6,230 less than their male white counterparts. Black females earned only $360 less than her white counterpart.

Earnings with: Four Or More Years Of College

Black Males
$31,380
Black Females
$26,730

White Males
$41,090
White Females
$27,440

Black males earned $9,710 less than their white male counterpart. Black females earned only $710 less than her female counterpart. This is a strong indication that black males are too economically passive. Black women can not help but get angry when black men so willingly accept such disparities. Black women cannot understand how the man that she is supposed to look up to--the black man--can insist that he is "the man" when he is functioning at a sub-standard level in comparison to white men.

Showing what black men do with their time, based on a Census Bureau study, released, June 24,1992, black businesses account for a measly three percent (3%) of all businesses in America. The U.S. total for business reached 13.7 million with blacks owning a mere 424,165 of those businesses. With black men owning 63 percent of black owned businesses, black women owned nearly half of all black owned businesses in America. The top three states for black owned businesses were California, New York and Texas. White men owned sixty-four percent (64%) of all businesses in America, with women owning approximately thirty-three percent (33%). From experience, black males are quick to moan and groan about the overall lack of economic power within the black race, yet most black males consider themselves "too cute" to start and maintain businesses.

In the seventies, when I begged and pleaded with several black males to open grocery stores, most complained that "the white man" won't let me. In 1992 upon encountering young black males and suggesting that they own grocery stores, they suggest and insinuate that owning a grocery story would not be "fashionable" or "cool" enough to maintain their pretentious "on top of the world," "I'm so pretty" egos and attitudes. I found another article to be of interest that appeared in the Detroit News, on Thursday, September 19, 1991. This article described the results of a Census Bureau report. It compared the earnings of small businesses in 1987. Small business earning receipts for white men averaged $189,000. For men of Asian-Pacific Islander origin, average receipts were $107,000. Hispanic men with small businesses had receipts of $66,000. Black men with small businesses had receipts of $50,000. American Indian and Alaska native men, had receipts of $47,000. Black men faired just $3,000 more in receipts compared to Indian and Alaska native men.

As a black woman, of the nineties, I do not even know of any businesses owned by Indians or men of Alaskan descent, nor do I even read or hear of them. (although in 1992 I read about the gambling industry, that is growing, that are slated to be built on Indian Reservation across the U.S.) Black women cannot help but wonder, how the black male can so aggressively *present* himself as strong, deliberate, socially aware, arrogant and totally together when white males out-perform black males in every single arena of life accept in sports. In 1991, Evander Holyfield at 60.5 million, Mike Tyson at 31.5 million, Michael Jordan at 16.0 million (Michael Jordan listed at 35.9 Million in 1992) and George Foreman at 14.5 million topped the list of the twenty highest-paid athletes in America.

How and why is it that white men earn so much more than black men? The same scales that measure black and white women are nearly, equally balanced. Black women were forced to establish themselves as independent and self-reliant as a result of being "left alone and single" by the black man's decision to not marry and or divorce. Black males, females and most importantly, black children could enjoy better life standards if they collectively and unconditionally commit, strive and work toward improving the overall plight of black people in America. Though black women have been successful in obtaining equal pay in comparison to white women, women in general earn less than men in similar job positions.

Earnings By Occupation and Sex
Median Weekly Earnings

	1990 Men	1990 Women	1991 Men	1991 Women
Managerial	717	507	741	519
Technical	494	329	498	351
Service	317	231	320	243
Production	487	319	488	354
Laborers	379	262	391	275
Farming	262	214	269	220

In the seventies, as black women were establishing lives for themselves, the Women's Liberation Movement resurfaced to focus on yet another new generation of women--entering adulthood. The voices of this "Movement" told all women across the country--"educate yourself, assert yourself, strive for success, equality--be all you can be. Seek new heights! Reach new heights! Success! Equality! Success!" This "Movement" served to motivate all women. It encouraged women to believe in themselves. The Women's Liberation Movement set out to establish and acquire equal rights for women on the job, in the home, in politics, education, etc. so that they could maximize their potential to excel and enjoy all that life has to offer.

Hundreds of books were written to aid women in building mental, spiritual and even physical strength. In follow-up just as many books were written to teach women how to best use their newly acquired strengths and opportunities. A woman could get a book (with her as the main focus) on any possible subject from cooking to finances, communication, to getting and keeping a husband. Obviously, it was not only the black woman who was being alienated by her counterpart--the male.

Choosing different paths, it seems that black
males left their women to party while white
males left their women to "collectively"
acquire wealth and power.

No time to waste time, ambitious and impatient
black women took advantage of the new-age
freedoms and opportunities out of boredom and
raw curiosity. For whatever the reasons, black
women became wiser and more knowledgeable
about themselves and society. Black males
failed to recognize, the significance, benefit,
and importance of informal education, social
awareness and experience. Young black males
were not talking (about anything) and worse,
they were not listening (to anyone). [Much
like many of the young black males 16-35 of
the nineties who will fall prey to negative
social outcomes and statistics, unless they
change.] Unlike, uninformed black males, the
black female realizes the advantages of
substance and purpose in one's life. In the
early nineties, I asked a black male friend who
is "heavily" involved in politics, what was the
main agenda of his political affiliation. His
flippant reply was, "to get re-elected."

The black woman desiring to add "meaning" to
her living and character learns who she is,
what she wants, what she stands for and why.
Usually, if a black woman comes across as
confident and sure, she is. (Except for the
black females who become influenced by other
socially, fraudulent, perpetrating blacks) In
the average black male's opinion, confidence
in a black woman is a negative attribute. A
black man, very close to me once told me that I
spoke with too much confidence in my voice.
My tone of voice had reflected the *EXPECTATION*
for us to be successful at what we were doing at
that particular moment. Hurt and, I quietly
slipped away in painful, quiet tears. (The

83

sensitive "one" that I am") Though loving him
still, I was later to learn that black men get
very angry in the face of female courage and
strength, that they lack but pretend and wish
they had. Black women have an extremely
difficult time trying to cope with the black
male's two-part personality--the man he
pretends to be and the "male" that he is.
Unbeknownst to many black males, there is a
big difference between a male and a man.
Black males are known to erupt in painful,
violent rage as they struggle to define and
understand themselves. Behind a thick shroud
of arrogance and resentment, black males
conceal their lack of security, understanding
and knowledge of the basic skills necessary for
development into manhood.

The fact that black women cannot understand,
why black males feel they cannot openly
share, with them, their feelings of frustration
and anger is very troubling to black women.
The black woman, inwardly feels sympathetic
toward the black male who does not and can not
realize that he fools no one but himself in his
attempts to *appear* satisfied, happy and
successful. To no avail, the black woman often
tries to assist the black male in dealing with
his deficiencies and shortcomings only to have
him lose himself to frustration and self-defeat.

In defeat black males become angry, first with
themselves and secondly with those closest to
their immediate environment, thus black on
black crime. And lastly the black male vents
his anger against the system or society at
large. In anger, black males, (like some black
females) will cease all communication and
thought about personal growth walking away
from challenging situations or dilemmas--
sometimes for the rest of their lives. The
"sensitive" and emotionally fragile people that

84

they are, black males finds "problem solving" difficult and frightening. If solutions to problems do not come quickly and easily, black males, just as "quickly and easily" succumb to defeat.

Unafraid of change, ambitious black women do not fear the unknown of new experiences or the inevitable challenges of everyday life in America. As a black woman, it is my perception that black women are more likely to subject themselves to social challenges more readily than black males because most women are comfortable with asking for the assistance that taps them over the top of barriers...that place them closer to the goals they set out to reach. The black man who has become a "victim" of our "quick and easy" society, sees no real need to exert himself beyond that of recreational activity, to set and reach goals just "inches beyond his fingertips. A common attitude among black males is that "if it cannot happen quickly and easily" it must not be meant to be" as he strolls away in "typical," PROUD, STRONG, ARROGANT AND (OH SO PRETTY) black man "style." Black males simply shy away from "things" they have to "figure out", such as things that have no common everyday, run-of-the mill formula like 1+1=2...a practice that black males must change if they are to survive as members of the human race. If black males "collectively" have no desire to change the way they operate, everyone can just SIT BACK AND WATCH AS THE BLACK MALE WILLFULLY SELF-DESTRUCTS. (Anyone for popcorn?) (Just kidding...the plight of the black man is NO laughing matter.)

If nothing more than intuitively, the black woman knows that empty, unsubstantiated, arrogance is not a healthy attitude, for survival, especially for a black male in America. Life experiences, positive and negative, teach black women that meaningful and worthwhile achievements do not come without positive expectations, commitment, discipline, ongoing formal and informal education and work. Accomplished black women have come to firmly believe that positive thinking and productive action will almost always produce positive RESULTS.

Proud and excited about her own successes, the black woman often finds herself "running after" the black male in futile attempts to push him toward just "one" extra mile in getting what he wants, regardless of the obstacles and challenges. The sad and ridiculous outcome is that "the chase" is mistaken for something totally different, by arrogant black males. Egotistically driven, black males assume that is is his irresistible sex appeal that attracts a black woman to him. It seems, it never occurs to a black male that a black woman might see untapped "success" potential in him, perhaps because it is difficult for black males to recognize their own "success" potential.

A large majority of black males find it very difficult to seriously and personally consider the issues vital to better than average, successful living. Secondary, to having a good time, are the issues of employment, growth, financial security or financial independence. Though black males are quick to agree that they are socially oppressed, few are willing to take any real initiative in correcting the problems that mostly plague black males. In 1992, I find it alarming and frightening, that in quiet, reflective moments, black males almost always cite recreational activity as their most significant, motivating forces in life.

Hence, the black woman struggles to determine if she can love and most important to the black woman, respect a man that runs from success, growth, legitimate self-respect and quality living. The black woman struggles to determine if she can be happy with a man that has become content and comfortable in immensely enjoying "basic freedom" and "basic opportunities" as opposed to "slavery". When black males are asked how they are, they will usually rely, "GREAT," "FANTASTIC" "COULDN'T BE BETTER," even if they lack transportation, employment and $5.00 in their pockets. The black woman wonders, does her counterpart really believe that he is equal to other men, realizing that statistics show otherwise. Contrary to what black males believe, black women will always love black males, for yes, they *are* beautiful. However, more than anything else BLACK WOMEN WANT TO RESPECT BLACK MEN, not because they are supposed to, but because black males respect themselves, each other, black females and black children, giving them no choice in the matter because black men warrant, earn and deserve the respect of black women. Unfortunately, in 1992, such is not the case, though the black woman strives to re-establish the love and respect in the black family and race that was once everything and the essence of the black race.

Perhaps the black male is just falling in line with American cause and effect. When America attains the best, America also attains the worse. For instance in America, (compared to other Countries) America ranks number one in big homes and number one in homelessness. America ranks number one in highest-paid athletes but last in teacher salaries. America is number one in bankers and number one in

87

bank failures and bailouts.   America is number
one in Fortune 500 international companies,
but also number one in Fortune 500
international companies that lose money.
America is number one in corporate managers,
but last in growth of industrial productivity.
America is number one in leniency toward
drinking while driving and number one in
drunk-driving fatalities.   America is number
one in percentage of young people that say
premarital sex should be avoided, but number
one in teenage pregnancies.

So maybe it stands to reason that since the
abolishment of slavery, overly blatant, racial
discrimination and segregation the black male
has become lazy and complacent.   I guess it
also stands to reason that since gaining
"acceptance" as a man, he has lost a great deal
of pride and respect in himself, as a man.   It
also seems that, more than ever before, the
black male shows less respect, appreciation
and loyalty to the black woman and his
children.   Some black males, treat some black
women as though they do not "deserve"
respect, appreciation or loyalty.   In general,
some black males balk at showing even the
slightest bit of courtesy to black females and
black children...a tragedy that keeps in place
the oppression, pain and suffering of the
entire black race.

Having a counterpart so out of focus with
"racial" realities as they influence life-long
living, causes increased self-doubt frustration
and confusion for the black female.   Seeking to
rid themselves of all inner-turmoil, ambitious
black women aggressively seek to better
themselves.   In this regard, black males do just
the opposite.   Defiant and angry with
everyone, resentful black males make
"negative" choices to become more

irresponsible, aloof and non-productive. Black males, known to pout, further alienates the black woman because her agenda is not in sink with his. Immaterial is that fact that the black male's "agenda" may not exist or that it is negative to growth or any type of quality living standards. Black women often find that it is a definite struggle to succeed in life while loving a black male. With this, more and more black women across the country struggle to keep their dreams alive, as they set out to prove, at least to themselves, that they are worthy individuals of all that they may desire and seek in life, as black males flow in and out of their lives.

Black males, generally, establish for themselves a solid false sense of self-worth that they feel needs no mental or spiritual growth or support. Thus black males can usually maintain relatively consistent demeanors and temperaments,thus maintaining an "air" of arrogance and success regardless of how bleak their lives may be. The pride that black males erroneously cling to makes them feel as though they need no development in the areas of self-esteem, self-awareness or even self-discovery. Hence, a vast majority of black males are unwilling to honestly determine how they feel about themselves and why, as they wonder aimlessly through life. Thus most black males are unable to cope with the one problem that angers and frustrate them the most--themselves. For this reason, black women (in the nineties) suffer from a "shortage of functional black men" because so many black males end their lives before they ever get started either by social defeat, anger, imprisonment, drugs, or unnatural death.

As companies and corporations complied with equal employment opportunities, black women consistently entered the workforce in increasing numbers...as black males went in other directions. Black males complained that though companies may have endeavored to hire more blacks, they did so reluctantly and discriminately. It is the black males theory that as companies satisfied their "minority quotas" they did it with a twist. In that a minority is either a black person or a woman, companies figured out a loop hole that left black males, as usual, standing on the outside looking in. Companies figured out a way to kill two birds with, one stone. In hiring black women, companies satisfied minority requirements in two categories with one employee--the black woman. Black males, thus feel cheated by the system and by black women in this regard. Gainful employment a major factor in economic strength, black males often feel justified in their anger and resentment toward the system and their counterpart--the black woman.

When black women revel in the strides that they have made in establishing themselves as functional, responsible and self-supporting adults, black males feel that a good majority of black women have done so on the backs of socially down-trodden, black males.

The careers of black women have developed in almost all areas of the workforce, from professional to technical. Black women find themselves established as professionals, as well as blue and white collar workers. Some obtain skills in electronics, drafting, computers, dentistry, medicine, law, and politics. Some black women obtained government jobs in the areas of service, i.e., postal service, police protection, and social work. Gainful employment has allowed black women to feel the comfort and appreciation of knowing that

they have achieved a level of financial
security, stability and personal
accomplishment that spur them on to higher
heights..

Black women feel very proud of their
accomplishments. They feel a sense of pride in
themselves as worthwhile and valuable,
contributing individuals. Black women feel
pretty good in knowing that they have
successfully entered into adulthood, with a
strong sense of self, responsibility,
independence and achievement. As a result,
black women, feet better, look better, they are
better.

Black women represent a significant
percentage of the workforce among black
workers on most levels. Black women account
for, in total 50.6%, of blacks in the workforce.
Professionally, black women account for 63.8%
of the black workforce; managerial level,
55.0%; technical level, 62.6%; blue collar level,
27.6%; military officers, 20.5%; enlisted
personnel, 14.5%.

Black males forced great numbers of black
women out into the workforce, as not all
wanted careers, causing the adverse effect of
fewer jobs for black males. Some black women
would have been *more* than happy to stay at
home as mothers and wives, as some males
chauvinistically proclaim, "where a woman
Should be." But no, black males stated to the
black woman, "you are no better than me,"
"you are just as strong as me, you are going to
work." Thus, black males robbed themselves
of jobs because of their unwillingness to
marry and support black women and their
children.

91

So off to work black women go, making great
strides in the fields of their endeavors of
which they are very proud. BUT, there is a
missing element in the lives of many black
women. Black women are functionally pained
by the disappearance of the "functional" black
man in their lives. Dealing with the loss, the
loneliness and the "games" of dating, black
women must primarily rely, first, on their
inner strength to proceed in life. If fortunate,
some black women can also rely on one
another for moral support as they enter new
territories of greater success and achievement.
More and more, successful women are
personally learning and making the statement,
"yes, it is true, success is nothing without
someone to share it with." PUBLICLY admitting
to this problem for the black woman is, no
doubt, embarrassing for some. Nevertheless
the black woman is very sensitive and serious
about what she needs. Most will agree that
they want black "MEN," not males, (there *is* a
difference) who can enhance, support,
appreciate and contribute to what she has
accomplished or plans to accomplish, for the
positive benefit of all parties directly
involved, for the positive benefit of the black
race, and the overall positive benefit of
mankind.

Positive, is what one must be if one is to be
successful in life. And I agree with Ross,
Perot, a self made billionaire, that says that,
*success is doing something you enjoy and
doing it well* and the best *way to measure
success is in terms of personal accomplishment
and personal satisfaction.* However, knowing
some angry people, regardless of race, creed,
age and sex, they will arrogantly say, "I am
satisfied being unemployed, drug addicted and
totally dependent upon others. These are the

92

people that need help in finding the courage
and strength to face the truth about
themselves...but there is still hope, if they
want to help themselves.

Many black women sadly accept and realize
that in many cases "the average black male" of
the nineties has chosen or will choose a route
to destruction. As a black male, which route
will you choose? As a non-black male, which
route will you choose? As a person, regardless
of race, sex and age, which route will you
choose? It is never to early or too late to
choose, prepare and work for success in life.
White, males another significant part of
American society, share in some of the same
self-destructive problems as black males. White
males share in the rolls that fill the statistics
of males who commit violent crimes, males who
abandon their children, males that are
illiterate, males that accept the status of being
unemployable and males who self-destruct by
drug addiction or default--wrong choice--
wrong place--wrong time=death.

I was able to personally experience the painful
destruction of a black male whom I thought
was a man, but, he too, like many other black
males never realized "true" manhood. He
meant a great deal to me and many others who
knew him. I first met him, when I was
seventeen. We remained extremely close until
I turned twenty-five or so. He was four years
older.

From what I knew of his past during his high
school days, he was somewhat of a scholarly,
bookworm kind of guy. He was President of the
Student Council, a member of the Honor Society
and as I recall Captain of the football team. If
I am not mistaken he even received an athletic
scholarship to a major university. Between us,

93

there was mutual love and respect. Because he was older, I looked up to him. In subtle ways, I worshipped him. At the time, it felt good to be nice, quiet, obedient and passive for the "guy" that I loved. When we met, I lived at home with both parents. In High School, I was not employed. Upon graduation, I went to a Business School. Upon completion, I returned to my home town for employment--which I secured.

With earning power and its benefits (money) I did not change my attitude toward the role "my place" that had been established for me in my relationship with the only man with whom I have ever known true love. As he had a tremendous number of "friends," it was usually one big party. Once in preparation, for a weekend trip, one of his friends told me to get in a particular car. The reply of another friend was, "she won't move unless *he* tells her to. This was true. I knew, accepted and liked my place, as "his woman." I was learning about womanhood relative to being a good woman, or so I thought. I was pampered and treated very well, as a lady.

At twenty-two, because of gainful employment, I began to learn about the mechanics of being an assertive, responsible conscientious adult. The make up of my personality possessed a natural childlike innocence. For some reason, he begin to tell me to "stop giggling." "Stop smiling so much." "Grow up." Because I wanted to be a "*good*" woman, I changed my behavior to suit his wishes, taking on a more adult-like persona. As it is still heard in the nineties, I had heard that some black male's preferred white women, because of their agreeable, unchallenging natures. I put forth a subtle effort to be extra agreeable, giving and sweet. He never asked to marry me.

94

On several occasions, he tried to talk me into having a child for him. Being only twenty-three, and still quite naive and immature, I asked him who would care for the child, as I knew I was not yet qualified to be a good mother. He never said, "we would." He said my grandmother could take care of "our" child. To me, this did not sound right, coming from a man who wanted to "become a father"—or "father a child."

In my own mind, I began to question, the reasoning and rational behind the thinking of the guy I loved. I began to observe his decision making process, his sense of responsibility and his personal direction. All of a sudden, the partying and good times were not so much fun anymore, especially after four years of it with the same people, at the same level, with no apparent progress or growth or talk of it, that I could see or speak of.

Looking back, (in my own opinion) I was very weak "as a woman." I had never learned, nor desired to be domineering or manipulative. At twenty-three, one question began to plague my thoughts more and more. "Can I put my life in this man"s hands?" SHOULD I put my life in this man's hands, as I thought we would always be together. The more I watched and observed him in every day life, the realization occurred that I was afraid to put my life in his hands, though I loved him dearly. The relationship ended!

He went his way and I went mine. From what I heard, he continued "living it up with his friends." I also continued to enjoy life, but by mere association, subconsciously and unintentionally, my life became "career oriented." In my heart, I still loved him, but we drifted further and further apart.

After about two years of separation, I began to
hear rumors of substance abuse about him.
The rumors seemed to come more and more
frequently. I ran into him a few times. Each
time he looked tired and slightly worn. He was
not progressing in life. Because of "the place"
that he had established for me, coupled with
the respect I had for him, it was impossible for
me to question him about his lifestyle. I could
not accuse him of the rumors about substance
abuse. Black males often subtly and
subconsciously force black women to quietly
watch as they self-destruct.

He and I talked from time to time expressing
the love we had once felt for one another and
had found in no other. I continued to progress
and grow in my career and as an adult. He
seemed to be regressing, going backwards,
standing still...at best. Many of his friends
were no longer as strong as they had once
appeared to me. He could not seem to pull it
together, but I still loved him and I still had
come to love no other man as I loved him. I got
stronger, my "career" was flowing in a positive
direction. In a quiet, reflective moment, one
day, I felt that if I could somehow make enough
money to support us, I would marry him.

After about four or five years of separation, we
began to try and get together for breakfast. I
called him on one particular Sunday morning
for breakfast. He told me that he could not
meet me for breakfast because his cousin had
just died from an overdose of drugs.

About a month later, I went to breakfast with
my Mom. Upon my return, I noticed messages
on the answering machine. I laid down for a
second or two. I said to myself, "I better see
who has called me." I listened. It was his
voice. He said. "Call me, Cherry." When I

96

called, I was told by his sister that he had been
found behind the wheel of his car. He had died
of a massive hear attack! He was about thirty-
seven or so at the time, in 1989. Could his life
have turned out differently? Is there a
possibility that he could still be alive today?
Was his early death a result of the route he had
chosen for himself?

So often the black woman is faced with this
question about the black male's of our society.
Every year, by the hundreds, the lives of black
males are destroyed as a result of unnatural
death or crime. Or to a lessor degree they
willingly render themselves "socially"
dysfunctional, far too vulnerable to death and
destruction.

In 1980, DEATH due to homicide took the lives
of four-hundred and seventeen (417) black
males in Detroit alone. This figure was
increased from only one hundred-ninety seven
(197) in 1960. By 1986 this figure jumped to
five-hundred fifty-three (553).

In 1987, the Adult State Prison Inmate
Population claimed two-hundred sixteen
thousand, two-hundred sixty-two (216,262)
black males. Twelve-thousand, four-hundred
and fifty-seven (12,457) of Michigan's black
males were incarcerated. It costs about $22,000
per year to house an inmate, according to the
Michigan Department of Corrections. In
Michigan alone, in 1987, over a quarter of a
billion dollars in taxes were required for the
incarceration black male inmates.

Many black and white mother's of America
wonder where the tax dollar is spent. Why is it
that black children, in particular, are not
afforded quality educations? The billions of
dollars that are spent to house clothe and feed

97

black and white males of crime could and should go to educate, clothe and feed the children.

Here is what just a few states had to spend (out of our tax dollars) on jail expenditures to house, clothe and feed convicted criminals who are, no doubt "worry free". In 1988, New York, spent $872,290,000; California spent 659,718,000; Florida spent $360,767,000; Illinois spent 106,562,000; Michigan spent $128,311,000 and South Dakota spent $5,061,000. Why do so many males choose lives of crime, imprisonment and early deaths over successful living? Maybe they *are* successful in that the criminals in just six states are GIVEN a budget of more than *two billion dollars* affording them living standards better than some people who go to work everyday, earning honest livings.

And worse, veterans who have fought in DEFENSE of America in wars like that of Viet Nam are rendered homeless in *their* inabilities to cope with the consequences of war related emotional and physical problems. A federal Task Force on homelessness shows that of the 600,000 homeless people in America on any given night, approximately one third are veterans. It is not fair that criminals are afforded billions of dollars to provide them with comfortable, clean and warm lifestyles for the crimes that they commit *against* society...while veterans suffer in the cold...hungry and delirious with no place to lay their heads.

An article in the Detroit Free Press Newspaper by Deborah Barfield, on Wednesday, July 29, 1992 stated how "the government and Congress have been slow in reacting to homeless war

98

veterans," by Rep. Lane Evans, D-Ill. Re. Evans cosponsored a bill that would provide $48 million to expand services to homeless vets, while convicted criminals remain comfortably housed, clothed, clean and fed, better off than millions of children who are raised in poverty who have committed no wrongs against anyone, in their young, innocent and fragile lives.

In the United States, in 1960 one million, four hundred forty-thousand, one hundred forty-two (1,440,142) black males were unemployed. By 1980, this figure jumped to two million, seven hundred ninety one thousand, one hundred eighty nine (2,791,189). In 1980 in the Detroit area, ninety-five thousand, twenty-four (95,024) black males were not in the labor force. WHY?

The black woman has just cause to be angry, confused, and frustrated. She cannot help but wonder how the black male has allowed himself to become a mere "victim" of all possible social ills. The black woman realizes that with the available, positive opportunities as they have existed since the sixties, there is absolutely no intelligent excuse for the destruction that the black male has caused himself, negatively affecting the black family structure, black children, the entire black race and society at large.

The black woman is angry...very angry and frustrated as well. The black male has been separated from her for so long, that he is in 1992 afraid of the mere "thought" of communicating with the black woman. It angers the black woman that the black male chose chooses to "party" rather than except the responsibilities of marriage, family and manhood. The black male chooses to go to an extended party that often turns into violence, unemployment, drug addiction, poverty imprisonment and eventually early death.

For this reason, the black woman, alone shoulders so much of the responsibility in maintaining the pride and dignity of the black race. In many cases, the black woman acts as mother AND father of the black race, assuming the dual roles of strength and quiet softness, simultaneously. Because the black woman has become so accomplished in learning HOW to survive, the black male deprives the black woman of what she seeks most from him--love and support.

In spite of himself, the black male deprives himself of the life he deserves but has not the courage to accept. Though it was hundreds of years ago that the black man was once considered, less than a man, sub-human, inferior to other men, shiftless and lazy, it is the "modern day" black male that followed that maintains and nurtures the stereotypical adage that the black man is worthless and no good...for anyone, not even himself.

BUT more importantly, it is the black man and woman of the nineties who must work HARD together, to reclaim and re-establish the pride, dignity and excellence of the black race...that will successfully survive and prosper for many years to come.

CHAPTER TWO

THE COURAGE TO FACE THE TRUTH

The black woman of the nineties feels better about herself. She knows what she wants and how to go about getting it. The black woman knows and understands what drives her and what motivates her. She strongly feels and believes she deserves all that she desires and more.

The black woman, of the nineties is destined to succeed and is willing to WORK for what she feels she should have, sometimes regardless of how long and hard she must strive AND work to satisfy her needs and wants. She has come to realize, that if she wants something bad enough, the reward is well worth the effort. Black women who find themselves alone (single, unmarried, unattached) accept responsibilities for making success happen for themselves. In 1992 Oprah Winfrey, was noted by Forbes, as the entertainer with the most earning power. As a TV host and film producer, Oprah Winfrey earned 46 million dollars, out earning Bill Cosby, Steven Spielberg, Michael Jackson, Madonna, Johnny Carson, Prince, Arnold Schwarzenegger, Eddie Murphy, Stephen King, Sylvestor Stallone, MC Hammer, Frank Sinatra and Janet Jackson. There is a part of Oprah Winfrey in every single black woman on the face of the earth.

Though a significant number of strong black men in America have become very successful, the black male who continues to believe that he is destined to fail, simply because he is black will do just that...fail.

101

Black American males who are told they must pull themselves up by their bootstraps, even without boots, who want, need and expect to succeed, WILL succeed in life, far beyond their own expectations and against all odds if they are willing to work hard at achieving the level of success that they desire, deserve. hope, wish and dream of.

Unlike successful black women, the endangered black male has no belief and true confidence in himself. Far too many black males do not know who they are, where they have been, where they are going and why, let alone how to get to their chosen destinations in life.

Sadly admitting the truth, far too many black males are expecting to live and die as failures. Though much of society encourages and contributes to the destruction of the black male, black families and the black race must shoulder much of the blame for destroying the manhood of the black male in America. Black mothers are telling black males, their own sons, in the home that they are "worthless," "no good," and "useless" just like their fathers. Black mothers are instilling in their own black male children that they will grow up to fail. Black mothers are depressing and oppressing their own son's and some of their daughters long BEFORE their world's take them into white, mainstream society. Black mothers must encourage their children to succeed.

Black males easily settle into foggy states of existence. Progress and growth is not a part of the black male vocabulary, mindset or lifestyle, who has willingly accepted personal failure and thus, social failure. Black males who have been convinced that they will fail are willing and waiting to fail because they are expected to fail by their mothers, their fathers, friends, later to be joined by the rest of society.

Because thousands of black males are born and raised on pathways to destruction, many black males come across as lacking in substance, direction or concern for their own well-being. Causing further harm, black males learn to disguise and hide their deficiencies behind the curtains of arrogance and "male bonding."

Black males, no doubt, feel deep inside their hearts the excellence that they should be expressing and presenting, but because of negative stimuli all around them, in the home, the media and black communities, black males are encouraged and allowed to present and resemble all the negative aspects of their characters and environments. Compared to the days of slavery, whites no longer oppress blacks. Blacks oppress themselves and each other in the worse place and most effective way of all...in the mind, in the home, in the family, in the community and throughout the black race.

Black males, bewildered by the persevering survival of the black woman, believe that life in America is much easier for the black female or woman. Life in America is *not* easier for the black woman who wants to succeed. Black females and women, who seek success in life, make life easier for the themselves. Most black women will agree that they have had to face the same obstacles, roadblocks and barriers as the black male. Black females, will agree that they are forced to lift a lot of the same social weights as black males. The weights and obstacles of discrimination, racism, intimidation, just to name a few are

just as heavy for black females as they are for
black males.

The difference between the successful black
female and the black male who succumbs to
defeat is that the successful black woman
decides NOT to be a welfare recipient, a drug
addict or prostitute, or an illiterate. Black men
and women, who do not and will not fail in life,
decide for themselves not to fail in life.

Forced to be strong the black woman is still
capable of being the type of woman that the
black man NEEDS to help him survive; though
many do not realize it. The black male must,
realize that the type of black woman that he
thinks he wants no longer exists. Black males
want the woman of yesterday, without
excepting the responsibilities of men of
yesterday.

Overcompensating for one of the most common
complaints of many black males, that the black
woman is no longer "good" for the black male,
the black woman of the nineties is better and
so much more than what black males allow
themselves to realize and appreciate. The
black male must stop crying, arguing and
fighting about the change in the black woman
that has rendered her independent,
opinionated, confident and ambitious. The
black male himself put an end to the role of
"housewife and mother" for the black woman.
Assuming the exclusive role of housewife and
mother is an option and privilege very few
black women can enjoy in the nineties because
black males are unwilling to work hard enough
to financially support a family and household
consisting of husband, wife and children.
HOWEVER, if black males wanted, believed and
worked to be fully functional husbands and
fathers, they could recreate the type of

104

relationships and families that they fantasize about. Black MEN can do anything they want to do. Black males, however complain about what they cannot do without putting forth the necessary effort to achieve particular outcomes.

The problem with the average black male is that he does not want to succeed because it is so much easier to fail especially with the way that the black family structure has relaxed it's expectations of adherence to discipline, respect, social values and self improvement. Black women who have the slightest desire to succeed in life, seem to have more of the necessary courage to set and reach goals. For instance, with my inexperienced efforts to write, I am *trying* to write a best-seller. A male counterpart who is also writing, stated that he is *not* trying to write a best-seller. The difference is that I have the courage to succeed, as well as the courage to accept the possibility of an unsuccessful attempt to write a best-seller.

Although many black women have and will continue to achieve varying degrees of success, it has not been easy, contrary to what black males want to believe. Males and females of other races are no doubt aware of the obstacles faced by black women, as they themselves may pose as obstacles and roadblocks.

In may of 1992, a white, fifty year old male co-worker exclaimed to me that he indiscriminately, discriminates against everyone. In his own ignorance, he admitted to his own personal insecurities and deficiencies, though he himself is technically skilled and proficient in his profession...but not at much as he desires to be. As with most dangerously, insecure individuals, they find it much easier to kick others rather than legitimately work to achieve higher intelligence and self-worth. Successful black women realize and rationally deal with obstacles, posed by others, without hostility, rage, hysterical anger, or defeat. Successful black women realize that there is no such thing as an obstacle, only alternate routes.

Having the courage to venture into mainstream society, the black woman is familiar with "the system" and how it works, as well as how it does *not* work. Because there are many "gray" areas within the system, social systems, rules, regulations, mechanisms, institutions and entities are always subject to change to better fit the needs of "the people," most often those in power, authority, control or significant wealth.

The black woman, seeking to set and reach goals, learns the art of negotiation and compromise to her own advantage and benefit. It is apparent to her that, though society may expect for her to accept a level of inferiority, it is not acceptable to most proud, black women. With a healthy attitude, the black woman realizes that all cannot occupy the same space, level or status at once. So, to her advantage, the black woman carves a niche for herself in society, that is satisfying and comfortable to her. Or better yet the black woman *creates* her own niche or status. For the black woman, this is success. Note Oprah Winfrey and Whoopi Goldberg.

If others regardless of race or sex, including the black male could understand the basic attitude of the black woman, and accept the black woman as the valuable and viable member of the human race that she is,

106

mankind could and would be more effective in curing more of the ills that plague the black race that trickle within and throughout the entire human race and world.

Some racists bigots, who find themselves "hating" blacks might say, get rid of all blacks, and the problems of the world would be solved. Realistically and intelligently, most thinking people know that ridding the world of a race of people would not be a viable solution to solve the problems of mankind in that the troubles of mankind lie within the troubled hearts and minds of individuals, more angry and frustrated with themselves than with any other person or people on the face of the earth. Ignorance and fear separate human beings from the courage to face the truth about our own strengths and weaknesses.

In 1992, I had two older white men state to me on two separate and isolated occasions that "white men are the worse creatures on the face of the earth." Many blacks and whites would agree, that whites have made some tremendous contributions to mankind, however whites have also contributed to the destruction of much human excellence through systematic racism, discrimination and oppression.

A parallel, an article appeared in the Detroit News in November of 1992, entitled "Ashamed To Be White: *Pop star* Paul Simon *is outraged that the man who killed his Graceland colleague Headman Tshabalala won't spend a day in jail. Tshabalala, a member of the black South African vocal group Ladysmith Black Mambazo, was shot to death Dec. 10 by a white security guard, who was sentenced to five years-two years suspended and the other three to be served under house arrest. "This is the sentence for murder,"* Simon *told the New York Daily News. "This is an insult to Headman's family, as if his life has no value. But that's the way it is under apartheid. If makes you ashamed to be white."*

To Mr. Simon, I say that there is no need to be ashamed of what you are and your compassion for mankind, regardless of skin color is highly commendable. It is, however, paramount that all people in America and around the world strive to establish the true excellence, value and respect that every human life deserves and is granted at birth.

Additionally there are hundreds of thousands of whites who realize that they too are plagued with the same deficiencies, shortcomings and frustrations as those considered most inferior, namely blacks. Just like some blacks, there are some whites who are illiterate, socially dysfunctional, destructive, abusive, violent, lazy, shiftless and loud. Causing even greater frustration and anger, some whites find it absolutely IMPOSSIBLE to live up to the fallacy that, "whites are unconditionally perfect and superior to all other races, especially the black race.

Like most intelligent people, some whites are coming to realize and accept that it cannot be humanly, scientifically and logically possible for certain groups of people to be deemed unconditionally superior to others simply by the color of one's skin.

Whites appear more successful and accomplished because whites, collectively, work harder to make themselves stronger, smarter and socially powerful, thus they appear superior to those who feel inferior, a

108

fact blacks will have to acknowledge if they are to ever acquire social equality "for themselves." And of course there are some whites who realize that they can often ride with the tide of successful whites, with very little effort, education and achievement and still acquire a satisfactory degree of success because of their white skin tones.

The sad fact of the matter is that, while great numbers of whites and other racial groups are working and striving TOGETHER to achieve economic growth and strength...greater numbers of blacks are out partying or looking and waiting for the next party. The declining plight of the black race is a result of the declining respect and pride that blacks have slowly developed (toward themselves as blacks) since the mid-seventies.

If the plight of black America is to take a turn for the better, blacks must first of all look to themselves for inspiration, preparation, determination, enthusiasm and the motivation to turn their oppression and depression of the nineties into prosperity and economic security in the year 2000 and beyond.

Because blacks make up a small portion of the population in America, blacks are NOT the primary cause of the problems that plague a great majority of Americans as the twenty-first century approaches (contrary to what many people would like to believe.)

The problems in America are rampant and the fault of ALL people living in America. And until every single person in America takes responsibility for his or her own well-being as well as the well-being of other Americans, all Americans, will continue to suffer the ravages of aids and other diseases, hunger, homelessness, illiteracy, ineffective educational school systems, poverty, drug abuse, child abuse (sexual/physical), rape, acquired insanity, unemployment, racial war within itself (gangs), suicide, murder, abortion, crime, depression, discrimination and racism.

The problems that plague Americans are increasing as a result of the social band-aids applied to social wounds deeply infested with anger, hostility, ignorance and hate. With the help of untapped resources, like the black woman, America can do more in ridding American families, communities, schools, industries and society of the problems that can and will destroy America if all Americans do not collectively seek to change the way Americans think and act in every day life.

In order to survive, society is in dire need of ways and vehicles that will tap into the talents of those that are most socially disadvantaged, dysfunctional and disconnected. Americans must reeducate itself to realize and accept that all American citizens are individually and collectively responsible for creating the opportunities and benefits of life necessary for improved life standards. Far too many whites have socially, unhealthy attitudes and knowledge about the capabilities of blacks.

As a black woman working for a major corporation, sitting next to a sixty year old white man with similar job responsibilities, I was amazed at his "perception" of my sense of discipline and commitment. During a conversation about weight loss, I relayed to him that a male friend of mine suggested that I lose twenty pounds. His response to me was that I should tell my friend to make one hundred thousand dollars. He went on to imply

that it would be just as difficult for me to lose
20 pounds as it would be for a black man to
make one hundred thousand dollars.

My conclusion, of the conversation was that he
believed I lacked the commitment, discipline
and control over my own body to reach a goal
that I personally set for myself. As a black
woman, not only did I feel insulted for myself,
I also felt insulted for black men that he
insinuated would not be likely or capable of
making $100,000.

Society's overall awareness and use of human
resources, opportunities and capabilities fall
far short of what they should be to extract
maximized success because we expect one
another to fail. In fact, people are so
selfish,envious and insecure, that we often
want others to fail. If America is to survive
and prosper as a leading nation, all Americans
must expect success in all endeavors.
Americans must share the abundance of
knowledge that flows among us to find
solutions to the problems that stifle and
destroy the opportunities to live the wonderful
lives intended for us to live.

For instance on the issue of abortion...a very
troubling and controversial issue, much time is
spent as people ponder, what is right. Not
committing myself to be for or against it, there
may be a way for opposing forces to reach
workable solutions for all concerned. Being a
female, I have had occasion to lend support to
women who find themselves faced with the
dilemma of unplanned pregnancy. Under
certain circumstances, when abortion is the
chosen option, the female need not always
suffer the emotional trauma and other
negatives that surround a woman's decision to
terminate a pregnancy.

If the female immediately (within days following conception) chooses to terminate a possible pregnancy, the prescription drug called Prevera may be an option under the supervision of a qualified and licensed physician. Prevera--usually in pill form, one dose, five pills taken at once can be prescribed to a female patient when a menstrual cycle is late. Think of the tax dollars that could be saved that pay for "medicaid" abortions. The millions of dollars that are used to pay for the abortion process could aid in educating, clothing and feeding children in America who live entire lives of poverty and deprivation. (Of course, doctors might object, considering the medical cost difference) One prescription of Prevera is probably ten dollars or less.

In the United States in 1988, more than a million and a half abortions were performed. This statistic resulted in rating the United States as number one in abortions performed, higher than countries like, Denmark, Japan, Italy, Sweden, France and Canada. Reportedly, the abortion rate seems to be highest among young women, the poor and minorities.

Of all the women I know, I have never met one woman that was familiar with Prevera. Yet, almost every woman I know has gone through a complete abortion process. Americans must do more in educating one another, inside and outside of formal classroom settings. Americans, regardless of race, sex or age must aid in decreasing the over-abundance of idle, useless and idiotic chit-chat. Conversations about nothing must be replaced with pertinent and enlightening conversation, that will aid in creating quality living standards. Americans must strive to prevent unplanned, unwanted pregnancies that result in unwanted, abused and neglected children.

As all blacks are in the deepest need of improved life standards, black women, must reduce the countless hours spent, discussing men. Black women spend far too many hours trying to figure out what black males are thinking and doing in their absence. Black women must come to the realization that regardless of how much time and energy is spent thinking and talking about black males, (in their absence) your thoughts and conversations (about black males) are worthless in achieving the happiness and success that you seek in life. If black women spent, just half of the same energy talking about possible solutions to solve at least one social problem, the entire human race would benefit.

All Americans must seek to raise their conscious levels to realize the value of all human beings. When we can allow ourselves to understand and accept the full value of all human beings, particularly the black woman, we can then begin to take advantage of an idle resource that is waiting to be tapped, recognized, utilized and appreciated in her assistance to contribute to the betterment of all man and womankind. America has far too many problems to be solved by too few willing hands.

Too often, black leaders, want to point fingers and say, "You owe us." As a black female voice, I say "we owe ourselves." Sure government entities, corporations and some of American systems perpetuate and maintain the oppression of blacks that started during the days of slavery...that should and must be stopped if America is to survive. BUT too often

113

the disadvantaged, particularly blacks, are unwilling to share in the work to bring about economic strength and power within the black race. In 1992, there is no unity in the black race worth speaking of, let alone working with. Blacks must increase their sense of unity to bring about economic security and strength.

For overall lasting effect and benefit, blacks as of 1992, do not know how or where to start in working toward it's fair share of economic strength and power. Jessie Jackson must teach his followers to strengthen their own legs to stand on their own two feet. Instead Jessie Jackson continues to assemble the poor for new sets of crutches and bandages to once again "temporarily" heal the wounds of poverty each and every time socially disconnected individual slips between social cracks. And worse, there are blacks who claim to care about healing the wounds of the black race, yet half of the blacks in America walk around not even acknowledging other blacks, regardless of income or social status.

To aid in bridging economic gaps, it is definitely not my position to say that America has no need for affirmative action and improved equal governmental regulations. All Americans must continue to push for equality and equal justice until all people can understand, recognize, admit and work to eliminate the racism, anger hate and mental quirks that exist in the minds and hearts of most human beings regardless of race, creed or sex. Thus we all fall prey to unfairness and must keep a watchful eye on the actions of all men, women and children until values and morals are established that promote peaceful, just, harmonious, fair and prosperous living standards for all people in American and eventually all over the world.

If all of society suffers in small ways as a result of the pain and problems of others, why is it that Americans cannot bring themselves together, to solve all problems, individually and collectively? I question if people really want to solve social problems of crime, drugs, corruption and deadly disease. Are some people so selfish that they want everything to themselves, leaving the masses to suffer in agony and pain? Are you one of those people? Have YOU come to the conclusion that there are not enough valuable resources and assets, so you are willing to harm others in YOUR efforts to achieve success or basic survival? If this is so, we obviously do not realize, that each and every member of the human race, is an individual storehouse of unlimited treasures and talents.

In EACH of us there is a presidential candidate, life-saving doctor, corporate executive, supreme court judge, Whoopi Goldberg, (actress, entertainer, former welfare-single parent), Michael Jackson singer (entertainer), H. Ross Perot (self-made millionaire, 1992 presidential candidate) Oprah Winfrey (millionaire, Talk Show Host), Sam Walton (self-made millionaire), Vanessa Williams (Miss America, singer), Bill Gates (computer genius, wealthiest man in America, 1992 at 36) Martin Luther King Jr. (Civil Rights Leader), Michael Jordan (basketball player and businessman), Joe Girard (listed in the Guinnes Book of World Records as "World's Greatest Salesman"), Terry McMillan (best selling, black author), Donald Trump (one of world's richest people in business), Ernest Hemingway (famous author), Calvin Klein (world-class designer), Arsenio Hall (actor, talk-show host), Steven Spielburg (movie producer), Eddie Murphy (actor, comedian), Olympic Champion, Spike Lee (movie producer) or even Cherry Scott

115

(aspiring author, automotive designer, entrepreneur), waiting to be unharnessed and channeled for full expression for the purpose of making a better way for yourself and others. Racism, discrimination, bigotry, envy, prejudice, insecurity and ignorance will one day destroy mankind's most precious and valuable commodity...human excellence.

Have you allowed someone or even society to convince you that you are worthless, inferior, mediocre/average with absolutely no star potential? Or, rather than searching within yourself to find and develop your own star, do you find it much easier to tarnish, stifle and block the efforts of others to make your own star appear larger and brighter than it actually is, whether in the community, classroom, boardroom, workplace, basketball court, or just among family and friends?

Or, is it just plain "OK" by you to waste whatever talent you do have by living in a blank, meaningless, state of existence, contributing nothing to improve your own life or the betterment of mankind as those before you have done, for you? How does it make you feel to watch others make thousands or millions, while you sit back and stare in awe, with your only comment being...Woow! Think about it.

How much of your time have you wasted watching others fully develop and present themselves? How much more of your life will you continue to waste in useless and meaningless activity as others pass you by with capabilities equal to yours? When will you realize that the difference between those that succeed in life and those who do not, does not lie in talent or intelligence, but in commitment, discipline, hard work and expectations to succeed?

Yes, you might say, that "I would LIKE to determine and establish my own star potential." But, you might ask, "what does "personal success" have to do with understanding and accepting the value of others? Everything, because no one can ever fully define, understand, establish and develop their own self-worth in its entirety until one is able to appreciate, accept and understand the worth of others--particularly the talents of blacks. *If you cannot allow yourself to recognize the worth of others, it is your own unsatisfactory "lack of worth" that you are in fact failing to recognize...*personal insecurity.

To deal with our insecurities, we lie to ourselves and others in an effort to create a false sense of greatness to ourselves in all out efforts to win or give the impression that we are winning. Blacks, especially must stop giving the impression that they are winning. Black males must stop wearing the five and six hundred dollar suits, with no money in their pockets. Blacks must stop buying the expensive cars, jewelry and clothing while literally homeless and jobless. Black mothers must stop buying the most expensive clothes for their children while on welfare and living in shelters.

Wanting to win is a natural part of human nature. Pretending to win or simply giving the impression that one is winning is not the answer or way to success. From another angle, a great number of people want to win so badly that they are willing to destroy the potential of others because they have convinced themselves that they can only win by cheating, stealing, lying and robbing others of

117

whatever human assets and resources another person might leave unprotected and securely embedded in the mind and heart. Everyday people set out to rob others of self-esteem, self-confidence, hopes, dreams, in an effort to win in the game of life.

Not realizing that greatness is built on the foundation of past, present and future, universal excellence (energy) most people do not realize that destroying the potential of another, will in fact stand to destroy one's own potential for maximized excellence and greatness. Significantly, if a person chooses to destroy the potential of another person to succeed, this person has destroyed a level of his or her own potential, in that we are all unique, in possession of unique mental capacities, capabilities and awareness of great universal value. Thus, the very essence of what you may destroy in another may be an element that may be essential to your own maximum success or to that of the human race.

We all must allow ourselves AND others to determine, establish, develop, nurture and present maximum potential in relationships, education, the workplace, politics, social issues, nationally, locally and internationally. It SEEMS that it is the intent of mankind to discover and put in place workable, effective solutions to solve the problems that plague our societies. But, until, we rid ourselves of selfishness, personal insecurity, envy, sexism, and racism to unconditionally allow all people to "actively contribute" to the society of which all mankind is a part, we all will randomly, continue to feel the pain and misery of corruption, disease, illiteracy, abortion, poverty, violent crime, drug addiction, racism, physical abuse and more.

Most, social problems develop out of anger, frustration, personal insecurity, selfishness and racism as we block others from acquiring maximum love, wealth, peace and happiness. Thus we block ourselves from the things we want most in life. When you rob others of love, peace, money, happiness and maximized prosperity, you eventually lose what you have stolen, when you need it most.

To reach our fullest and highest potential in our personal lives and in society all people must identify, recognize, acknowledge and change the actions that deprive others of their opportunities to excel in life for the maximum benefit and survival of mankind.

If we are the men and women that we "think" we are or will become, we must honestly identify and question our feelings of insecurity, envy, frustration, prejudice and racially motivated behavior and actions. Most of us will come to realize that it is not the next person who falls short of the perfection we envision and seek. The imperfections that we hate or detest, lie mainly within own own hearts, minds and actions. We ourselves, Americans and all other human beings on the face of the earth are responsible for creating and causing the personal and social tragedies that we see and experience everyday.

Using well-known and well-established examples, everyone is or will become aware of, discrimination, bigotry and racism in America. Discrimination, bigotry and racism stand as barriers between harmonious relations among people and the success that most of us seek in life. Established and maintained primarily by those in power or authority, discrimination, bigotry and racism is used primarily against those who have no power or are not a part of

119

the majority. A world-class problem, racism, discrimination and bigotry is used to maintain control and strength over those who are seen as threats to the "sense" of superiority that others have created in their minds, hearts and institutions built to protect that same power, control and authority.

In America, when one thinks of discrimination, racism or bigotry one might automatically think of the relationship between whites and blacks in America. And most would agree that whites are apt to discriminate against or show racist type behavior toward blacks or other races classified as "minorities." Though the instances of discrimination initiated by those in power is a prevalent and troubling problem in American society, discrimination is also a serious problem within the black race. Racism is more than a black/white problem. Racism in the nineties is also a black on black problem, initiated by blacks, used by blacks, against other blacks to separate, alienate and oppress, just like a racist white person.

For the same reason as whites or others in the controlling majority, some blacks in the nineties discriminate against other blacks to create a sense of superiority or to maintain a degree of control or power over other blacks. Racism or discrimination within the black race, nothing new, was prevalent during the days of slavery between blacks who worked in the house of white masters and those who were relegated to work in the fields. Racism within the black race in the nineties might occur between darker and lighter skinned blacks, blacks with kinky hair verses blacks with straight hair or between blacks who deem themselves successful verses blacks who are less fortunate.

120

In that some blacks liken success to integration, becoming entirely surrounded by white associates and friends, some blacks try to disassociate themselves from blacks in efforts to convince themselves that they have become as white as humanly possible, for a black person. For some blacks in America, success is defined by how white their environment is. A black person in America who signals that white is right, better and the ultimate achievement, proclaims that yes, blacks are inferior and undeserving of racial equality.

To secure a newly acquired position or status of "crossing over," some blacks intentionally alienate other blacks to maintain their positions of being "a different kind of black person" or "special black person" (unlike the others). It is extremely important to point out that racism, an action, a thought or a statement used to alienate others based on racial affiliation, is a false and pathetic way to validate one's own value and self-worth. Skin color or hair type are two physical characteristics that in no way can determine or influence intelligence, physical abilities or emotional compassion.

Because employment determines one's financial status, discrimination, racism and bigotry are most harmful and destructive when used or demonstrated in the workforce or business world. Though it is apparent that blacks must learn to accept more responsibility for their own financial well-being, it has been proven and documented that blacks are most likely to be subjected to the ravages of racism and discrimination in the workforce, where it is likely to hurt them most in life.

121

Though one is able to deal with emotional or mental pains as a result of racism or discrimination, the economic pains caused by racism and discrimination are much more difficult to overcome as one's economic strength or power impacts on almost every single aspect of life in America.

Black men, are placed at automatic disadvantages before they even enter the workforce. It has been long established by whites that black males are more difficult to work with in the workplace than black females. The impression that black women assimilate easier into mainstream society provides another reason behind the strife between black men and black women.

It becomes very difficult, for a black man to live or effectively interact with a black woman, especially if the black man is unable to obtain gainful employment. As most black women do realize, it becomes very hard for black males to legitimately consider themselves men in the full meaning of the word, when their counterparts, black women, become sole providers of food, clothing and shelter.

As a result of racism, blacks are more economically depressed because, in the nineties (for the most part) blacks are still last hired and first fired. However blacks must take part of the the blame for their economic depression in that they do no establish and run businesses to even partially support the needs of black employment. As stated in the book, Two Nations, by Andrew Hacker, it has been established that white America has ensured that black Americans experience double the rates of unemployment as whites in America.

UNEMPLOYMENT RATES

YEAR	BLACKS	WHITES
1960	10.2	4.9
1969	6.4	3.1
1970	8.2	4.4
1979	11.3	5.1
1980	14.3	6.3
1989	11.4	4.5

So regardless of whether it is the black male or the black female who is shut of of the workforce, the entire black race suffers as it is systematically determined that blacks will NOT be afforded the opportunities of gainful employment at twice the rate of whites. But blacks must not feel sad and sorry for themselves. Blacks must strive to establish, maintain and most importantly SUPPORT black businesses to gain economic strength for themselves as well as to contribute to the job market of which all mankind must depend for economic strength and survival.

In the mean time, black women, must take advantage of all opportunities to acquire satisfying life standards. However, black women are still apt to be subjected to discrimination and racism in the workforce, especially where pay is concerned. Black women, along with white women are paid below what males are paid (black and white) though they may hold identical jobs with identical responsibilities.

Black women, determined to succeed in life, enter the workforce and function within self-imposed perimeters until she locates for herself a comfort zone as she accesses the environment, which is likely to be predominantly white, from management, to

123

supervision, to entry level staff. (Especially within major corporations.)

Some black males, aware of the realities that racism and discrimination does exist within "the workforce" refuse to place themselves in the position of being "the only black person" in the workplace. With preconceived notions, some black males, choose welfare over being supervised or managed by "a predominantly white establishment."

A significant factor that also separates blacks, both male and female from the workforce mainstream, is in the areas of appearance. Some black males and females, alike, refuse to adopt outward appearances that coincide with "the professional" or "business" environment. Surely it is logical to accept that some cultures in America call for differences in self-expressions in clothing and hair styles. However, a significant, self-inflicted barrier for blacks in the area of self-presentation lie in the fact that blacks unnecessarily over-present themselves in clothing, hair and personal style.

For black females/women wanting to assimilate or mainstream into the workforce, it must be realized that three-inch nails, polished with bright, bold colors is inappropriate and unprofessional. Big, and flashy hairstyles, like those of entertainers, is also inappropriate. And clothing that is disruptively, revealing or fitting, i.e., after five or evening formal apparel is also inappropriate for the workplace. Additionally, rings on every finger is also a signal that could be used against black females applying for gainful employment.

For black males attempting to enter the workforce, expensive suits, coats and shoes that make you appear wealthy, as you apply for a $12,000 a year salary position, does not do much in showing your NEED for such a job as you present yourself in a $1,500 outfit with lizard skin briefcase to match. Black males would also do themselves a favor in wearing haircuts that do not resemble abstract paintings to better blend with business establishments. Flashy and gaudy gold jewelry is also unacceptable. Since society is becoming more casual, big floppy, unlaced, athletic shoes and the hip pants are also inappropriate for young black males seeking employment.

Though black males and females are sometimes reluctant to comply with dress codes and the "norms" of self-presentation in the workforce, they must come to realize that in the refusal to 'adapt," they willfully subject themselves to welfare and poverty for the sake of a dress, hairstyle or attitude that should be left to times and places wherein statement-oriented apparel is the norm or more appropriate. No doubt there are people of other races, white, Hispanic, etc. who also deprive themselves of opportunities as they refuse to conform to established and acceptable social norms.

If black men and women would establish and operate more black owned businesses they would be less apt to be forced to comply with the white rules of a white company. When blacks start to own more companies and businesses, there will be more jobs for blacks to set and function by rules set and enforced by blacks.

Black women, with the courage to fail or succeed, bravely enter the workforce with quiet enthusiasm, and a purpose...a purpose to succeed when she is often expected to fail. Not often does the black woman begin a new job opportunity with an aggressive "do or die" attitude in an all out effort to "immediately" out perform her co-workers, as she knows whites are sometimes easily threatened by outward displays of excellence by blacks.

When society speaks of the word mainstream or assimilate, the words can have a two-fold meaning. Whites speak of a black person's ability to enter into the mechanisms of American life with the least amount of difficulty or interruption of the natural flow.

In actuality, a black person's ability to mainstream, in many instances, depends upon one's ability to APPEAR "as average" as possible while actually producing twice as much as a white counterpart and being able to accept credit for doing less than what is "actually" contributed to a task or operation, which, in and of itself, is a subtle, but very real, disappointing and disturbing form of discrimination.

Nevertheless, the black woman's desire to be successful in life, usually means that she must become successful at earning a living for herself. Unless circumstances change, the chances are very slim that a black woman will become a housewife of a husband who accepts all responsibility for providing shelter, food, clothing and all the other amenities that provide for satisfying life standards.

Along with the financial rewards, a black woman's decision to enter the workforce serves also as the acceptance of the challenge to impress upon herself and others a positive impression that may aid in eliminating some of the negative images that society has about the

126

black race in general. Additionally, job experience for black women is used as validation of personal self-worth and confidence to forge ahead in setting and reaching new goals.

On the job, most black women are able to present themselves in a manner that is not defensive or threatening. Although occasions do arise wherein blacks are given cause to become defensive when whites blatantly show surprise or even anger for a black person's display of discipline, commitment, intelligence, social awareness or overall professionalism or diplomacy in handling uncomfortable situations.

As an example, in a one-on-one conversation (in the workplace) with a white male co-worker about the variety of dogs available for pets, I felt, without a doubt that this person intentionally set out to degrade me or make me feel bad about being black.

When a conversation turned to that of larger dogs, such as German shepherds, the white male co-worker of fifty, somehow found it necessary to say, "German shepherds were the dogs used to attack blacks as they fought for civil rights." Not exactly angered by his statement, I was shocked that he found it very easy to display his bigoted, racial ignorance, in an effort to make me feel bad about a painful part of American Black History.

I likened his comment to, if when in conversation with a Jewish person about micro-wave ovens, I could stoop so low as to say, "you know, those things that they put you guys in during the holocaust." I could never stoop so low to display such uncompassionate racial ignorance in an effort to cause pain to someone of a different racial background who had no control over what that person's forefathers may have suffered.

To deal with the white-male co-worker, unashamed of showing such low level ignorance and racism, I, unconditionally stopped ALL unnecessary conversation with this person. Blacks that do not in some way deal with racial slurs or negativity in the workplace encourage whites to continue there attempts to validate the perceived or supposed "inferiority" of blacks.

Blacks that do not discourage racial defamation (especially in the workplace) are often referred to as "toms" as they validate, accept and encourage the maintenance of negative stereotypes about blacks. Though blacks that do NOT discourage such behavior from non-blacks may pain very deeply from racial negativity, they (toms) feel that the pain of racially caused pain does not outweigh the of notion "being accepted." (by whites)

Blacks, who are referred to as tom's by other blacks fail to realize is that when they (blacks) do not diplomatically discourage racially derogatory behavior/statements/actions from non-blacks, particularly whites, they (tom's) aid in maintaining the negative stereotypes that have been established about blacks. Tom's, as referred to blacks, who talk white, act white and no doubt want to be white are under the misconception that other blacks are jealous as a result of their "perceived" pretenses to be white.

It is not jealousy, but anger and disappointment that some blacks feel toward Tom's as they are not self-respecting enough to be black in the face of non-blacks, to say, (verbally or non-verbally through dignified behavior) yes, I am black AND that makes me no less intelligent, capable or deserving of respect...And further, the blacks who some would label dysfunctional are just like me, with one difference.

The difference between, socially, functional and dysfunctional blacks, lies in the fact that, though I am black (not white) I was afforded opportunities and experiences that PREPARED me to better cope with life in America, as opposed to blacks who find it difficult or impossible to cope with the effects of a racially diverse society.

Blacks must realize that they could have, very easily been the little black boy or girl who was born to the poverty stricken, single-black mother, uneducated and addicted to drugs who could not prohibit the deprivation of her seven children, fathered by seven different men who never sent a dime to the children or showed their faces in the home...rendering most of the children hopeless and angry with society.

If the black race is to improve upon the plight that encompasses and effects all blacks, blacks must "collectively" realize that no blacks should look down upon one another as blacks are shunned enough by non-blacks. Blacks must also realize that when non-blacks look down their noses at dysfunctional blacks, they are in fact looking down their noses on all blacks as we are all the same, different only by our environments and lucky or unlucky by time and places of birth...just as with EVERY other single human being on the face of the earth regardless of race, sex, creed or color.

Apprehensive and reserved in demeanor, black women are often forced to consciously, ward off racially derogatory conversations or behavior that may lead to tension or interruption in the natural flow of the workplace. Unlike her white female counterpart, black females are aware that circumstances may arise at any time wherein a non-black co-worker may feel the need to "test" her for racial sensitivity.

As most blacks, are sooner or later faced with uncomfortable or unwelcome racial conversation or behavior, most blacks will agree that the occurrences must be dealt with sincerely, with a degree of firmness and dignity to ward off further negative racial incidences. Dealing with any uncomfortable or unwelcome situations in the workplace or any other place be it in the home, school, etc. should be dealt with tactfully and diplomatically to keep relationships free of hostility, animosity and revengeful anger as all people must live and function, together, whether we want to or not.

Because a black woman or female is usually a very small minority in larger companies, it is not a rarity for her to feel a slight sense of isolation. Especially in entry level positions, there is often a lack of support, encouragement, guidance or direction for black females. For black females determined to succeed in life, they accept the fact that they must rely on their inner strength and pride to overcome trouble spots and obstacles, without anger, hostility OR a desire to quit. For successful black women, the THOUGHT of failure does not exist. Failure lies only in one's own failure to try! Anyone willing to try and try again is successful.

Hundreds of thousands of blacks have been severely damaged by their own inferiority complexes as statistics, theories and conclusions are rendered almost on a daily basis proclaiming the shortcomings or deficiencies of blacks in America.

Blacks who proudly, embrace the fact that they are proud of who they are and worthy of all of life's opportunities, pleasures and riches, set out to challenge and destroy negative expectations and stereotypes about blacks. Self-respecting blacks, first of all eliminate all negative or demeaning thoughts that they may have allowed themselves to feel or ponder, emotionally or mentally, before setting out to present themselves as self-respecting and deserving of respect from others.

Blacks destined for success, establish and maintain positive attitudes, early in their lives, that they are inferior to no one, while recognizing that though they may not always win or rate highest among others, they grant themselves the right to work toward success and excellence in their chosen endeavors...whatever they may be.

Black females as they are saddled with the extra baggage of womanhood, must present themselves with pride and dignity in that a black woman is a minority with a two-fold status that can either work for or against her. A smart black person will CHOOSE, PLAN and EXPECT to benefit, rather than suffer, from that which he or she is and cannot change...black.

Any black person determined to succeed against all odds and obstacles can no longer stand to suffer from inferiority complexes or self-pity. Blacks, ready to face the challenges of full man and womanhood do so with pride, strength, discipline, determination and an overwhelming desire, commitment and will to succeed. As it cannot be denied that for blacks, success does not come easy as most people will also agree, regardless of race creed or sex. Success comes to no one who is unwilling to strive and WORK to achieve the successes that he or she may desire.

During the infant years of the black woman's career, she shows a natural and subtle level of confidence. She steers her personality away from the arrogance that her non-black counterparts may display regardless of her capabilities, strengths or experience. Because whites are supposed to be superior they may sometimes show signs of intimidation or discomfort when they encounter confident, intelligent blacks, disciplined enough to effectively handle job responsibilities and assignments. Through careful observation, black females learn the ropes/system of "the workforce" through trial and error.

Black women usually come to realize that non-black counterparts function from a significantly different vantage point than blacks are afforded. On the job non-black counterparts comfortably display lower levels of stress. (or none at all). Not being a part of the majority, can make blacks feel as though they are at times watching (from the outside) a family affair. Being a part of the majority lends itself as a "built in" support system. For whites "trouble spots" or "problems areas" are usually viewed as acceptable or non-existent by supervision or management.

This is NOT to say that employment, within a workforce whereby the majority of the employees are mostly white is an altogether unpleasant experience because it is not. The advantages of working for a large corporation usually far outweigh the disadvantages. Even with the imbalance of being the lone black person for every two hundred or so whites, there is much to be gained when one is a part of a viable and profitable company or corporation.

Anyone, regardless of race or sex fortunate enough to acquire gainful employment with a large corporation will most likely find the experience to be enlightening, educational and a financially rewarding experience. However as America faces the Twenty-first Century in an overall decline in all sectors of society, to acquire gainful employment with any company is a step in the right direction in restoring the American dreams that seems to be disappearing for many Americans, regardless of race, creed, color or sex. But an even greater step in the right direction toward financial independence and actively contributing to the American power machine would be for blacks to establish, own and operate more of their own businesses.

As American dreams and improved living standards, are no longer guaranteed to younger generations, concerned citizens, companies, institutions and policy makers are desperately seeking solutions to stop the decline of those "American Dreams." Among white employees, the feeling is beginning to prevail that management forces are not fully utilizing all available technical and human resources for maximized productivity. White employees, like black employees have felt for many years, are beginning to feel that they are insignificant to the "broad picture." Non-management and non-supervisory employees are beginning to feel left out, on the side lines of the major operations of which they are supposed to be a part.

In the nineties as companies report daily losses, white, non-supervisory employees are beginning to say, "if management is really concerned about reversing industrial decline, then corporations at the management levels must increase overall focus on base level employees to extract the opinions and suggestions of those who do much of the work. In like fashion, companies, institutions and government entities must also seek out the assistance of blacks, as they too are significant parts of the "social machines' that will restore and keep American dreams alive and strong.

Blacks, especially black women are forced into pigeon holes, as they are prohibited to fully excel in corporations established, owned and managed by whites. As most blacks will agree, there is an established and very real premise that blacks must be twice as good as whites to be considered, just HALF as good of whites.

No doubt causing frustration and quiet anger, blacks, especially black women feel stifled, unappreciated, insignificant and unimportant as they helplessly sit back and watch while companies ponder and question why, business is not as good as it used to be. After being overlooked and ignored, month after month, year, after year, black women come to recognize, how much of their intelligence and skill white companies are willing to accept or not accept for reasons of racism or sexism.

Unable to fully understand the reasoning behind the actions of "the powers in place," black women eventually realize that regardless of how much trouble companies, institutions and even black males seem to face in their

134

survival attempts, most find it difficult to accept, recognize and utilize an available and valuable resource...the black woman.

So as not to totally alienate themselves, some black women are known to apprehensively, display and utilize their true talents, abilities and strengths as a viable means of support to mankind and the societies of which black women are a very significant part. Though strong she is, black women of the nineties are very careful in their efforts to not appear overbearing or aggressive.

More and more black women are coming to realize that some non-blacks and black males alike are easily intimidated by intelligence and personal strength when attached to the female species. Intelligence is even more difficult to accept in a female, if she is black. The sad and unfortunate effects of racism and sexism, causes the ambitious black woman to sometimes hide or dilute her true capabilities and aspirations to fit the molds of what society expects of women and females. Even in 1992, in conversation with several twenty-one year black males, it is surprising to learn that these males have adopted the attitude that a woman's place is in the home, AFTER WORK, as many young black males are unemployed. These same, unemployed males, consider themselves men and head of the household.

The black woman, confused about her role in the black race and in society, seeks a comfort zone in functioning on the job with her co-workers and in her relationships with black males. More often than not the black female is given the impression that maximum performance by a black woman or female is prohibited and "unbecoming" of a lady, in the workplace as well as in relationship to black males.

Regardless of intelligence, strength or accomplishment, most black women feel that one's abilities and capabilities should not be connected to one's gender. Out of frustration, black males have a tendency to decrease the level of respect and appreciation for black women as they increase in intelligence or accomplishment. Hence, many black male's are comfortable in stating, "since you have the ability to think and positively utilize your thoughts like a man, I see no reason to treat you like a lady." Not resorting to such ultimatums, society, simply ignores the intelligence and strength of black women, whenever possible, though some talented black women refuse to be ignored or shut out behind the doors of discrimination, racism and sexism.

Because of the the black woman's desire to reduce and eliminate problem areas without sacrificing personal values and beliefs, she sometimes secretly or quietly continues to seek and achieve personal improvement. As black women are very much aware of the personal insecurities of others, some black women may choose to slowly reveal their true value, talents and capabilities so as not to alienate themselves beyond the causes and effects of their minority status.

On the other hand, some black women are so enthusiastic about life and all that it offers, they cannot resist the need to blatantly display their robust energies and desires to excel by wholeheartedly, thrusting themselves into life. These black women or young females, feel so confident and strong about their own destinies and personal beliefs that they freely propel themselves to excellence, totally disregarding

136

the insecurities and jealousies of others, realizing that they cannot stifle their own lives because others do not have the courage, strength, desire, discipline and fortitude to utilize and maximize *their* personal talents and potentials.

Personal growth does not usually prompt the black woman to become arrogant or lax in the workplace or in her personal dealings. Personal improvements provide the black woman with more confidence in knowing that she is capable of being successful. As the black woman realizes her own progress, she uses the progress as a foundation to enhance her ambitions, accomplishments and achievements. Personal growth for the black woman erases self-doubt as a result of negative opinions, stereotypes and suggestions associated with her blackness and womanhood. In the workplace, the black woman smiles inside as she realizes that her non-white counterparts surprisingly acknowledge her effectiveness and efficiency on the job, even in their reluctance to verbally express the acknowledgement.

Very rarely does the black woman or female receive the verbal or monetary praise and appreciation that she deserves or that her white female counterparts receive. Sometimes saddened and slightly disappointed, the black woman finds comfort in knowing that she has been instrumental in eliminating some of the worst negative perceptions that non-blacks have about the black race in general...that blacks are dumb, stupid, lazy, irresponsible and lacking in any type of self-motivation or self-direction.

Improvement in performance in the workplace by the black woman is usually acknowledged

137

by an eventual raise or promotion. The black woman feels and is often given proof that she is least appreciated and last on the list for promotions and raises, though she may out perform her counterparts. Studies have shown than most blacks, male and female are systematically "kept behind" their non-black counterparts in the areas of raises, promotions and recognition. At the very least, it may be verbally conveyed by supervision that improvements in job performance, have been recognized and or appreciated.

Black females entering the workforce must be aware that effective and increased job performance and responsibility should result in adequate rewards or recognition. Black females, because they are usually a part of a very small minority, are not aware of the monetary or promotional rewards that should be provided employees whose performances rank in above average categories. Whites, as they are in the majority, with relatives usually in the workplace, are afforded an advantage wherein they are made aware of what should be expected in terms of pay and promotions, simply by association.

Non-black supervisors are apprehensive in their interaction with some black employees, especially if he or she comes across as serious-minded, reserved and professional. Non-black supervisors admit to their lack of awareness in their interactions with blacks as their reasons for not knowing quite how to "deal" with black women in the workplace.

When blacks appear overly jovial and "happy go lucky" on the job, non-blacks seem to have an easier time in their interactions with blacks. However, to their own detriment, some blacks may have a tendency to go overboard in

138

"appearing" too happy and "carefree." This behavior, however can backfire, causing them to get just the opposite of what they seek most...respect from non-blacks and the acknowledgment that they are accepted as equal and quality human beings.

In the workplace blacks who paste perpetual "grins" on their faces in their attempts to get along and gain acceptance (from whites) often find that the acceptance that they gain is at the expense of their self-respect. Thus in their over- zealous attempts to become accepted by whites, blacks are, unfortunately accepted as still inferior, but now silly, clownish and overly agreeable...in line with negative stereotype about blacks. These same blacks further harm the black race in that they play into the stereotypes, established by whites that blacks are stupid and that they enjoy being stupid, especially in an effort to entertain whites.

Because certain blacks do feel that they are unwelcome in white "circles" they have a tendency to express with glee their happiness when "allowed" to be in the company of whites and that everything is r-e-a-l-l-y great. When blacks blatantly seek validation and approval from whites that they are at least OK, blacks reinforce the fallacy that whites are superior and blacks are inferior.

Hence blacks who are unsure of their own self-worth, significance and importance find themselves disrespected and devalued when they seek such validation from whites or anyone, outside themselves. Blacks with inferiority complexes, as well as all others must establish and maintain self-respecting, internal value systems that cannot be marred or destroyed by the NEGATIVE notions or

139

attitudes of others that may be negative to a person's overall well-being and personal growth.

Most people, regardless of race or sex will only respect people who carry themselves in ways that warrant respect from others. It is obvious to most that the people who unconditionally command the respect of others, first of all, demand of THEMSELVES a high level of self-respect. The person that functions from a platform of solid, unwavering, self-respect is confident and sure that they are worthy of all that life has to offer. Moreover, a person with a healthy and positive attitude has the courage and fortitude to set and reach the goals that they dream about.

Self-respecting individuals, already know that they deserve the respect of others, because they have established respect for themselves as a result of continuous personal growth, constant intellectual stimulation, self-awareness, social awareness, accomplishments a strong sense of integrity, commitment, discipline, values and morals.

As most black women are aware of the pain and degradation that goes along with one who has or shows no self-respect, most black women will, most of the time, try to present themselves with dignity and self-respect to keep others from getting the impression that disrespect would be acceptable. By establishing an initial degree of integrity and high moral standing with others, be it in the workplace, classroom or wherever, a black woman or female is most apt to ward off any future conflicts regarding unacceptable, disrespectable behaviors from others.

Nevertheless, even though a black woman carries herself in a dignified and professional manner, she is still likely to face undue tension and opposition in the workplace as well as in her relationship with black males. In the workplace, there are non-black co-workers who truly believe that blacks are inferior to all other races with "natural" deficiencies and capabilities in the areas of self-respect, commitment, intelligence, social awareness and discipline, as a result of being born black. What is even more significant is that non-blacks with unconditional, prejudging attitudes about blacks, want to hold on to their negative prejudged opinions and conclusions about blacks. Thus the non-black co-workers who have such negative, stereotypical, racially motivated beliefs about blacks EXPECT that blacks will "do the right thing" by showing themselves as irresponsible, loud, silly, carefree, careless, socially ignorant, socially deprived and EXTREMELY happy to be in the company of whites.

This is NOT to say that all whites or non-blacks possess negative, stereotypical attitudes and pre-conceived notions about all blacks. It is important, however, that blacks realize, that the impression that they personally leave with whites or non-blacks may be that persons first and only opportunity to interact with a person of color. Thus there are many non-blacks who earnestly want to become acquainted with blacks to gain insight to the racial differences that contribute to the whole of mankind. Gaining insight about the racial differences of mankind is the ONLY way that the wounds that separate, alienate and destroy can be healed to bring the changes that will preserve the human race and civilization.

When a black woman or female does *not* fall into the stereotypical perceptions of being "primarily" lazy, ignorant, fun loving, carefree and careless, some non-blacks as well as some black males become slightly uneasy. When non-blacks encounter black women who are intelligent, responsible, disciplined, as well as ambitious, racist non-blacks and sexist black males are put in a position to focus on the positive aspects of a person who is unconditionally expected to be inferior to all others. Thus feelings of tension, envy intimidation, resentment and even anger may surface in the person, who has hidden their unresolved feelings of insecurity and inferiority.

When it becomes instantly obvious that any particular, randomly chosen, black woman is in no way inferior to all others, racist and sexist individuals are forced to *secretly* look at themselves. Such a surprising confrontation, forces a racist or sexist individual to mentally measure themselves against the individual who is supposed to be, unequivocally, inferior to all other members of the human race.

A person who adopts, maintains and nurtures racist and sexist beliefs that they are superior to all others, simply because of race or sex does so in an effort to create and maintain a false sense of security and superiority that will hopefully keep them elevated above others, most importantly, in the "minds" of others. Most people who establish racist and sexist attitudes come to realize that their attitudes and actions are *not* for reasons of achievement or accomplishment. Hence the feelings of superiority that racist or sexist individuals are very fragile and weak. Thus it becomes overwhelmingly important that they convince, and keep convinced OTHERS that

142

they are superior even though there is no substantial, legitimate or intelligent reason as to why a racist or sexist individual should be unconditionally considered and accepted as superior.

As the workplace in America is the most common place where adults of different races interact, the workplace becomes a significant factor in discovering and uncovering the characteristics and fallacies that are associated with people of different races. As the black woman immediately disproves many of the negative notions that non-blacks have about blacks in general, it is not unusual for her to become a focal point in re-educating non-blacks about a significant member of mankind...the black woman...the black race. Even in 1992, a vast majority of non-blacks, find it surprising as well as disappointing that blacks are not exclusively a natural make-up of all human ills deficiencies and shortcomings.

Some non-blacks may even find the intelligence or worldliness of a black woman to be quietly, alarming. Black women, having a strong sense of awareness and sensitivity are aware of the surprise and alarm of others in their reaction to the unexpected quality nature and persona of a black woman. The black woman's reaction to the surprise of others may range from silent anger to insult. For the black woman long acquainted with her self-worth and confidence, there may be feelings of quiet amusement, as some non-blacks squirm in their insecurities fueled by a false sense of superiority. In a quiet moment she remembers that prejudgments are a part of her blackness as of the nineties. Relief comes for the black woman as she realizes that she has come to know her own strengths and weaknesses. The black woman is further comforted in that she has grasped the necessary courage to work with her own strengths and weaknesses in order to become the person she wants to be in the areas of work, compassion, talent, wisdom, experience, accomplishment and love.

Opened-minded, self-assured non-blacks are comfortable in knowing AND accepting that there are black women who are intelligent, articulate and hard-working. However, the non-blacks that are unsure of their own self-worth and abilities may experience extreme difficulty in accepting the intelligence and effectiveness of a black woman who appears equal in intelligence, competence and self-worth compared to a randomly chosen non-black person.

The non-black person who finds it difficult to accept any black person who appears just as intelligent, capable and accomplished as a non-black counterpart is imprisoned by racist thoughts and attitudes that will inevitably come to cause more personal harm than to the black individual. A racist or sexist individual functions and lives based on a belief that he or she is unconditionally superior, based on racial background, color or gender. Foolishly, a racist or sexist individual is a person who feels no real need for personal growth in the areas of education, personal awareness, accomplishment or achievement. Thus such an individual is easily overwhelmed by personal stagnation, frustration, anger, ignorance and hatred as he or she watches as those deemed inferior, prosper and grow...hence the angry bigot or racist.

While in the workplace, a group of fifty year old white males were discussing the process of obtaining a copyright. All parties confessed their lack of awareness for such a procedure. The white male that needed the information seemed to accept the information provided that he would have to pay approximately $2,000 for a lawyer to obtain a copyright for a project that he was working on.

Hearing the conversation, I interrupted with the information that copyright applications could be obtained from a local library, free of charge. I went on to tell him how simple it is to fill out an application for a copyright. Of most importance, I told him of the $20 processing fee that was much less than the two thousand dollars that he anticipated. He quietly and reluctantly, thanked me. Moreover, for the next few days it seems his expression toward me was that of a scowl rather than that of an appreciative smile for someone who had saved him two thousand dollars. In my opinion he was more disturbed that a black woman had solved "a white male's problem" than he was about paying two thousand dollars for a twenty dollar process.

Always eager to disprove the white supremacy fallacy to encourage racial harmony, in the midst of editing my book on an airplane, I decided to do a test of two intellects as I (a black woman) sat next to a white woman. We were basically the same age, give or take a couple years. Considering *myself* somewhat of a professional, from her appearance and demeanor, I assumed that the young white woman sitting next to me was a blossoming professional. Proving myself right, she told me of her newly acquired license to sell real estate properties. Being a former, licensed, real estate agent, I was very much aware that math skills are a primary requirement.

As our conversation led to the subject of nutritional habits, I told her that I drank so much "pop" in one year, that in returning the empty bottles I was able to collect seven dollars ($7.00). At ten cent a bottle, I tried to figure out how many bottles, I had returned. After some time I could not. After additional time, neither could she, (a white, female, licensed real estate agent who was soon to close on a one hundred thousand dollar deal).

Her husband, after looking at both of us in EQUAL disbelief, provided the answer to the simple mathematical equation. We both (one black, one white woman) just sort of chuckled. We both knew that this simple mathematical equation should NOT have been a problem, but it was. More importantly we knew our mental block, whether temporary or permanent would not keep us from becoming legitimately successful in life. For two women...one black, one white, this was a woman thing; for us anyway. It was not a racial or intellectual issue.

The aforementioned scenario was not to lessen the importance of math." "All education is extremely important!!!" However it is important to realize, that regardless of the barriers, obstacles or deficiencies, one must never stop believing in one's desire and will to succeed. Even as I had studied to pass the real estate license test, it took no less than five different men to bring me to a level of comprehending the mathematics of real estate sales. On the test, the math was the easiest and of all those men that tutored me, I was the only one who passed on the first try.

A national example was provided to all American people that one can reach the highest of heights regardless of one's

146

shortcomings if one has the courage and wherewithal to start and continue on a chosen journey to success.

Dan Quale, the Vice-President of the United States of America in 1992 prompted a twelve-year old fifth grader to misspell the word "potato" by adding an "e." The Vice-President of the United States of America attempted to rationalize his mistake with a Mark Twain quote, "you should never trust a man who has only one way to spell a word." Officials at the Mark Twain Museum in Hannibal, MO and it's library could not confirm the quote nor could experts at the Mark Twain Project at the University of California. This powerful example relays the message that regardless of one's handicaps or deficiencies, one must NEVER lose sight of one's dreams, goals and ambitions, even if one aspires to the highest of heights in America, such as a position in The White House.

And to top matters off in the area of achieving perfection *before* one realizes one's hopes and dream, Dan Quale, Vice-President of the United States provided America with another fine example to the contrary. (Monday, August 17, 1992) Vice President Quale, again, proved that one need not be PERFECT to actually realize high acclaim and achievement. While listening to Vice President Quale on the opening day of the 1992 Republican Convention, his position was that of "presenting" President Bush. As he addressed the sea of faces, assembled in Houston, Texas, he asked a question of the audience. He asked the Republican Conventioneers, if they had *seen* Bill Clinton's speech. (1992, democratic Presidential Candidate) A quiet hush fell over the crowd, as if they were unanimously embarrassed for the Vice President. No doubt,

147

everyone knew that the question should had been, "had they *heard* Bill Clinton's speech.

Thus, all people must realize that though it is important to be astute in all areas of education and sciences. Deficiencies should never stop anyone from hoping, dreaming, aspiring, and above all else, *working* to achieve the success, happiness, peace of mind and prosperity that is the right of every human being in America and around the world.

But as the year 2000 approaches, the great American dream is slowly becoming a nightmare. Happiness, gainful employment and peaceful living is becoming more and more of a rarity in cities across all across America. One would think that with all the high-tech intelligence and vast information and communication systems the American dreams would be guaranteed as humans have "supposedly" become more civilized, intelligent and worldly than ever before during the history of man.

Though still a super power among nations, American organizations, government officials, leaders, statisticians and private citizens wonder how did America come to experience such rampant poverty, illiteracy, violent crime, drug abuse, violent crime, budget deficits that the 1990's brought? There is but one answer to this question...an answer that few Americans are willing to acknowledge or admit to.

Americans are responsible for the demise and destruction of "life in America. Each and every single American citizen is responsible for establishing and maintaining the prosperity, peace and happiness that Americans *should* be experiencing in the nineties and beyond. But most importantly, it is all Americans, (each and every one) who must communicate and work together to restore the opportunities and possibilities for prosperity and peace that made America the greatest country in the world.

The decline in living standards and prosperity in America is the fault of individuals overwhelmed by personal insecurity. Individuals who define human value by skin tone and ethic background are the individuals responsible for the destruction of maximized potential in mankind. As value is put on the color of a person's skin or gender and not the content of a person's character, the very character and strength of America is destroyed by the ravages of racism, sexism and discrimination. Racism and sexism destroys the growth potential of those most vulnerable to social injustices. But unbeknownst to most racists or sexist minded individuals, those most apt to oppress become oppressed by by their own racist or sexist attitudes.

Individuals driven by unhealthy feelings of superiority, act as personal barriers to themselves. Just as a racist or sexist individual blocks the opportunities and possibilities of others, they too are blocked from the full excellence of mankind. Just as the runner who purposely blocks a competitor from a maximum performance...that same runner blocks the possibility of the *challenges* that could result in his or her *own* greatness or improved star quality.

Insecure individuals who are intimidated by the intelligence of others is a person who has an unhealthy attitude about his/her self-worth, value and potential to excel or succeed. Individuals drenched in feelings of insecurity,

149

intimidation and inferiority center their lives around the plotting of the oppression, persecution and degradation of those who show possible signs of the vulnerability or weakness. In America, blacks, as a whole, are most vulnerable based on their history in America and deficient gains in the areas of economic growth, stability and power.

A person driven by internal insecurities and inferiorities sets out to transfer their negative attitudes to anyone who is willing to accept the unconditional superiority of others. The transfer process is set up whereby a person with conscious or subconscious feelings of inferiority will take on an outward appearance of superiority. The transfer process is successful or complete when a person has convinced someone else that he or she is superior based on race, sex or even age. The ultimate value and harm of the superior/inferior transfer process occurs when someone has been erroneously convinced that he or she is less valuable and inferior to others because of skin color, race, sex or age.

It is not uncommon for a black woman to be subjected negative racially or gender motivated behaviors or attitudes especially on the job, as the workplace or business world is a fertile breeding ground for racism, sexism, discrimination. The strongest and tallest barriers between Americans and the full success they seek exists in the hands of racists who hold power positions in the areas of politics, financial institutions, large corporations and government agencies. Though less effective, barriers between Americans and full success, lives and thrive in the hearts and minds of people who maintain the hatred and bigotry that segregates, discriminates and alienates mankind from excellence through the oppression of others.

Though oppression for blacks once meant slavery and social segregation, the nineties has brought about a different type of oppression that is more subtle and less obvious for blacks in America. The workplace being a major part of life for most individuals, racism in the workforce/workplace is most apt to occur because the workplace defines and represents the quality of one's life and living standards. Thus, how one fares in the workforce or workplace, becomes paramount.

Regarding the masses, individuals employed with the large companies are most apt to gain financial security that usually provide for comfortable living standards. Individuals entering professional fields, such as in medicine, education, law or sciences are also more apt to secure quality living standards.

But, as most people want to be the best, experience the best and be paid the most competition among workers cannot be avoided as technology and world competitiveness continually decreases the opportunities for unlimited opportunities for gainful employment. In the nineties, there are not enough jobs, even among individuals who want to work. Those who are socially aware, realize the shortages of gratifying and satisfying job opportunities. Hence, more and more, people are easily threatened as they realize their living standards can decrease as a result of economic stagnation...smaller raises, no raises, no promotions, benefit cuts and job cuts.

For some whites, it is a common belief that affirmative action policies have afforded blacks opportunities for gainful employment that should have been reserved for a white person. And while some whites act as though blacks do not deserve the right of equal employment opportunities, these same whites are quick to complain about the numbers of blacks on welfare that their tax dollars are used to support. These same whites are also last to understand the anger of blacks as a result of economic alienation and depravation. However what blacks need to realize is that if their are to ever receive the full rights of equal employment opportunities, they must become equal employment EMPLOYERS!

However relative to the blacks that are employed by large corporations, institutions and agencies competition becomes detrimental to all Americans when gender or the color of a persons skin becomes a significant factor in the process of productivity, teamwork and positive results. Because America is often driven by race or gender, positive results often become secondary to preserving white or male supremacy and dominance.

This is not to say that all sacrificing of human and American excellence is rooted in racism and sexism because it is not. The problems of deficiency, lack and shortcomings among mankind lies within the basic nature of most human beings of the human race. For instance, within a family unit, the same feelings of threat, inferiority, superiority, intimidation and insecurity that can occur between strangers of different races can occur between biological siblings.

In like instances when a new employee is introduced to a department, other employees may feel that the new employee may be more effective, disciplined and committed to job responsibilities. If such is the case, it is easy to realize that the employee with more seniority may appear less valuable to supervision. It is easy to realize that raises may be smaller, the chances for promotions are slimmer and worse over, the single new employee may be able to do the job of two, resulting in the loss of employment for someone not yet ready to retire.

On the other hand when a new child is born into a family unit, older children may quickly realize that they may get less attention from parents who are now awed by the newest child. Older children may come to realize that parents are not quite as impressed by the actions of the older children as they are now amazed by the smallest accomplishment of the newest born baby. And causing the most harm, in the area of economic stability and security, older children may see a decrease in monetary gain as family monies are lavished on the needs of the newest born child.

Though the workplace and family scenario are different, they show that most problems among Americans and the human race can be traced to economic stability and security, regardless of race or sex. But this is not to say that discrimination does not occur as a result of race or gender differences because it does. All races, with the exception of the black race, seems to function within a common bond of unity and the acquisition and preservation of prosperity, dignity. Additionally males, regardless of race seem to function under a creed that maintains the preservation of male dominance. Hence there is still a great need for the policies and regulations that provide for equal opportunities regardless of race, creed, color or sex.

The workplace and family scenario show that the reasons behind tension, anger, discrimination and separation among mankind points to our quest for economic stability and security. Though unacceptable and harmful to all, it becomes, at least acknowledgeable that the reasons behind the subtle battles that exist in education, the business world and society at large are due to the fact that no one wants to be considered, associated or classified as the "underclass."

Because a classification of "the underclass" or "lower-class" usually means the worst and least of what life has to offer, Thus, a vast majority of individuals, institutions and systems either by race or social conditioning strive to oppress others to establish and maintain an underclass of which is clearly identifiable and recognizable. In most societies, the underclass is a shield, for the middle and upper classes, against poverty, unemployment, illiteracy, drug abuse, violence and social unrest.

To establish and maintain above average living standards, most racial groups collectively work very hard to become self-sufficient in satisfying daily personal and survival needs. It is only the black race, as a whole that falls far short in satisfying its needs in the areas of gainful employment, food supply, housing, finance and education for blacks.

Blacks, in the twentieth century, are not a self-sufficient race, hence, blacks detrimentally fall short of contributing to the satisfaction of social needs for themselves and society at large. Thus blacks, as a race, reap the smallest rewards in life though they were significant and major contributors in the founding, building, strengthening and maintenance of America. When white owned

and operated businesses fail to provide gainful,
employment, other races, particularly blacks,
should be able to satisfy the surplus of needs
in the areas of employment, education and
overall mainstreaming.

Although a vast majority of blacks see no need
to actively contribute to the betterment of
mankind there are a great number of blacks
who aggressively seek to position themselves
to make major contributions to improve upon
life standards in America and elsewhere.
However, the process for restoring American
dreams become unnecessarily difficult when
insecure individuals block the progress of
others out of envy, feelings of intimidation,
insecurity, inferiority, intimidation racism
and sexism. Racism first and sexism secondly
are two of the destructive elements of
excellence and prosperity in America.

In America the harmful effects of racism,
sexism and discrimination can occur in a
person's life as early as the childhood years in
the home, community or educational process.
A young person subjected to negative
behavioral actions and attitudes must somehow
glean from education, society, parental
guidance or personal insight that all people,
regardless of race, creed, sex or age are
entitled to equal opportunities, possibilities
and probabilities. Secondly, all young people
must realize that all life situations are not
always fair and equal. As life is not always
easy, challenges, obstacles, hurdles and
roadblocks must be used as weights to build the
necessary mental and spiritual muscles
necessary to achieve success.

As adults, most people come to realize that life
is not easy and the roads to success are
crowded, narrow, rocky and sometimes very

long. The doorways of gainful employment are crowded but those who enter the world of professionalism, skilled trade, corporate structures and business ownership find that they can relax *a while* as they have gained access to a vehicle on the highway of economic freedom, security and stability.

Feeling a sense of pride and relief, as the years of sacrifice, training and education pay off, a vast majority of Americans from the nineteen seventies up until the late nineteen eighties, find the transition into the workforce challenging, but not an impossible feat. But as babyboomers, people born between the "1940's" and "1950's" crowded the workforce, getting and keeping gainful employment becomes more and more of a challenge. As college educated young adults became somewhat of a norm, individuals who ended their educations at the high school levels, are pushed further down on the scales of status and pay in the workforce.

As companies strategize to remain competitive to stay in business, many exercise cost-cutting measures. Senior employees may be offered early retirements, younger employees may be offered "buy-outs" to sever all ties with the company, executive level employees may be requested to pay for the use of "company cars," benefit packages can be reduced particularly in the areas of health care benefits and time-off with pay can be reduced. Younger, entry level employees are hired at lower rates of pay. And with unions protecting the wages and benefits of non-professionals, thousands of jobs in America are lost as companies go to foreign countries, where the cost of doing business is much, much less than in America.

So with the threat of adverse conditions in the workplace some insecure or envious individuals may target a black female as a likely target for racism, intimidation, alienation, discrimination or the sabotaging of productivity. A decision to focus on the demise of another employee is in effect a decision to undermine the goals and objectives of the company for the selfish reason of destroying someone else to make one' self look better or fare better within the ranks of an overall employee population.

If a black female is subjected to negative behaviors and actions on the job, she is forced to concern herself, at least momentarily with a task for which she was not hired for. Possibly causing feelings of uneasiness or anger a black female is deprived of contributing at a maximum performance level.

If a black woman is positioned to work within the confines of a team effort, a non-black person may go so far as to withhold information or supply information that is wrong in an effort to harm the performance of the black woman. Black males are very rarely a source of comfort or support for black women in the workplace, as insecurity and resentment forces them to hold on to the belief that women belong in the home and not in the workplace. Discoveries or problems solved by a black woman may also be overlooked, especially if she works in a male dominated work environment.

Armed with the necessity to earn a living to stay off welfare, the black woman comforts herself with the belief that she has every right to earn an honest living in a way that is satisfying, fulfilling and growth oriented. The black woman also finds relief in knowing that she is well prepared to be a major contributor in the process of productivity that helps and keeps America strong, alive and well.

Not looking to cause problems due to unnecessary racism, sexism and the insecurity of others, the black woman strongly feels it is very unfair to have her performance level damaged intentionally by her co-workers. The black woman may say very little to protect herself as she does not want to come across as petty. The black woman often chooses not to relay small by annoying incidences to supervision or personnel for fear of being perceived as "part of the problem." For a black woman, because she could possibly be one of many, management may opt for her removal as a solution to a problem between employees, rather than dealing with the root causes of a problem that usually lies in the racist, sexist or insecure attitude of an employee with an unhealthy attitude about themselves and self-worth.

Remaining true to form, tension between a black woman and a non-black co-worker may be labeled a "personality clash." Because society, in general, has been unable to adequately address the more subtle problems, causes and effects of racism and sexism in America, life in America is becoming more and more strapped with more social problems than ever before.

The black woman finds the problems of racism and sexism in the work place to be disheartening in that she knows that problems on the job usually occur as non-blacks and some blacks as well become threatened by an effective job performance by a person stereotyped to be lazy, dumb, stupid and intellectually inferior to both white and black males.

158

A young black female just entering the workforce may find the insecurities of male counterparts, enlightening and just a little amusing. Through experience and perseverance the black woman, learns that though whites in America are socially and economically powerful, they are not, in and of themselves, individually far superior to others. In some instances, a black woman will go along with her assigned slot of mediocrity, as she realizes that white counterparts as well as some black counterparts seem to unconditionally overlook or ignore the contributions of the black woman on the job, regardless of the worth or value, especially in male dominated fields.

The black woman comes to realize that whites are socially powerful in America because they collectively commit and discipline themselves to set and reach goals that have long, range, positive effects on their freedom, pleasure, and economic stability and security. As encouragement for the black woman, she comes to realize that all whites are not unconditionally superior to blacks. Moreover, whites come to realize that they are not superior to blacks, though some may work very hard to maintain the fallacy of white supremacy.

For instance, most whites believe that had it not been for affirmative action, most blacks could never qualify to work in major corporations and companies. An article entitled "Affirmative Action Hires Perceived As Less Qualified," by Julia Lawler, appeared in the Monday August 31, 1992 Detroit News (a local Detroit, Michigan Newspaper) The basic premise of this article was stated in the first sentence. "*People hired through affirmative action programs carry a stigma of incompetence no matter how qualified they are for the job."*

Perhaps there are some cases where an employee hired through Affirmative Action may be deemed less qualified than white counterparts. However, after sixteen years in the workplace, possible affirmative action hirees (blacks) are no less qualified than the white sons, daughters, nieces, nephews, aunts, uncles, cousins and close friends hired by whites in positions of authority and power. Relative/friend-related hirees, as opposed to affirmative action hirees are, no doubt, less apt to fall subject to "established" procedural "qualification" guidelines. With this, if it were *not* for Affirmative Action, corporations and companies would be less representative of the society of which it depends upon for survival.

Additionally, a vast majority of whites like to point to minorities, particularly blacks as the root causes of declining productivity and quality work standards. To blame workforce ills on blacks is about as erroneous as unconditional, white supremacy. In 1990 blacks in America represent only 12.1 percent of the population with an 11.3% rate of unemployment, that represents 88.7% of blacks in America in the workforce. And of the 88.7% of blacks in the workforce, only 30.4% of blacks hold white collar positions, some with power that does not really exist.

Since blacks (as a race) represent such a passive and small percentage of the American population, blacks are not the driving or pushing forces that determine the success or failure of American life, business and industry. In the American workforce, a vast number of blacks represent untapped talent and resources overlooked by white power structures, while some whites represent unqualified, non-productive employees, protected and promoted, not by character or qualifications, but by skin color or 'an uncle or friend in the business."

Most blacks acknowledge and accept their lack of power and *recognized* insignificance in the American workforce. Disillusioned and disheartened, most blacks feel helpless in bringing about the recognition, respect and appreciation that they feel they deserve in the wage earning process. Far too many blacks settle into passive states of acceptance never realizing that they have the capabilities, talents and resources necessary to start and run businesses that would grant the freedom and security that most blacks only dream about. Hopeless, functional black males are known to state, "as long as I have twenty dollars and a job, I'm happy...while all around companies are chopping heads like weeds.

Reluctantly accepting the trials and tribulations of a black woman in America-- apart from black males and white America, the sensitive, ambitious and strong willed black woman continues to further improve herself in the workplace as well as in her personal life. The ambitious black woman in America is most likely to encounter problems with non-blacks who are less accomplished, disciplined and committed to self-growth and excellence. Non-blacks who present themselves as most unaccepting of an ambitious black woman, is also a person troubled by his or her own lack of ambition, self-worth and self-esteem.

A black woman who shows signs of ambition, determination, discipline, commitment and a will to succeed is threatening to a non-black who believed the fallacy that excellence or supremacy lies in skin color. An ambitious, intelligent and self-respecting black woman destined for success represents the fact and truth that excellence lies in personal growth, personal achievement and the courage to face the truth about one's self and others.

A troubled non-black individual will use the power of skin color to diminish, stifle, alienate, separate or destroy a potentially successful black person in an effort to maintain the fallacy that excellence is predestined by the whiteness of skin color. Blocked by skin colored ignorance, individuals who continue to define themselves exclusively by the whiteness of their skins, rob themselves and mankind of their own personal excellence. An attitude of white supremacy, simply by way of skin tone, is a sure formula for a lack of fulfillment and excellence by definition of character, personal achievement, growth and full development of personal talents, capabilities and intelligence for the survival and betterment of mankind and the human race.

A black woman may also be subjected to negative treatment and behavior from black males as well as other black females in the workplace as well as in other socially related encounters. In particular, it is not rare for a black male to feel threatened and intimidated by a black woman--his counterpart--who is intelligent, accomplished, ambitious, with a strong sense of self and success. The socially passive, soft-willed black male is most troubled by a socially and intellectually strong black woman because he sees in her what he himself should possess, but does not.

For instance, in the workplace, a black male counterpart, came over to my work station and asked how I was doing? I replied, "pretty good." He asked, "only pretty good?" I went on to say that I would not feel GREAT (as many blacks often *claim* to feel) until I had made a million dollars or made some significant accomplishment in my life. The expression on his face, came long before his verbal response. His face tensed and twisted as though I had silently passed gas, giving him no chance to escape before inhaling a putrid aroma.

His verbal response was that he was happy as long as he had twenty dollars in his pocket and a job. As the large corporation for which we both worked continued it's daily decline in job security, pay increases and benefit packages, the fellow who expressed no interest in personal growth or ambition, passed my way without so much as a nod in acknowledgement of my presence. His expression seemed to be that of emotional turmoil, self-disdain and disappointment in himself as he accepted such a voluntary, passive role in his own existence.

The show of ambition, discipline, commitment and perseverance in the black woman forces the black male to realize, acknowledge and accept his faults as a man who has no real power over his life, nor the inclination, drive, intelligence or courage to gain the power of a real man amidst the freedom and land of opportunity called America. Hopeless black males state with great ease, "this is a white man's world." Ambitious black women who dream, talk and work for greater levels of freedom and power over their lives remind black males that they are not the men that they are supposed to be--equal to all men.

Hence, the black male sees a strong black woman as a constant reminder or his own character flaws as a man. A vast majority of black males in America, driven by false pride and false strength, aggressively seek to run from rather than face their weaknesses and shortcomings in the areas of economic security and power.

Hopeless black males full of false pride try to distance themselves from black women of substance who desperately seek strong black men of substance. Even functional black males in mainstream America fall short of full manhood as they hide behind their powerless titles and positions in corporate America that can be wiped away in a millimeter of second rendering them no better off than the thousands of other black males blocked from mainstream America by slave mentalities and white power structures.

Instead of interacting with the black woman of substance, weak black males aid in isolating and alienating the black woman sometimes in an effort to further ingratiate himself with white power structures, just like the house "negroes" during the days of slavery. In 1992, fully aware that "blackness" still carries a stigma of negative connotations, most notably inferiority, some black males and some black females as well feel they will fare better with white power structures if they disassociate themselves with other blacks.

In a lot of cases the black male is quite obvious in showing his resentment toward the black woman's presence especially in the workplace. Some black males seem to give the impression that they can will the disappearance and absence of the black woman by totally ignoring her. By ignoring other blacks, some blacks give the impression that whites will either come to pretend or believe that "wanna be whites" *are* white or that whites will think wanna be whites to a special kind of black with no kinship to other blacks.

If a black male is extremely resentful of the the presence of a black woman he may go further in his attempts to belittle or discourage her confidence. For example, in the company of non-black females and black females, a black, wanna be white male, may shower the non-black female with compliments and flattery while totally ignoring the black females. Black males, have a tendency to bend over backwards with kindness and attention to white females while sometimes barely acknowledging black women on the job. The racially negligent and disrespectful behavior becomes a chief source of disrespect and or disdain for the black male from the black woman. The black woman knows that a primary definition of manhood for a man is his concern and acknowledgement of his women and children.

The black men in America (as a group) are considered least of all men in America because they do not adequately acknowledge or concern themselves with satisfying the needs of their women and children in the areas of employment, housing, clothing, food supply, economic security and power. To satisfy their needs for survival and those of his women and children, black males seem to have no problem in going to white men of power, discipline, commitment, strength, hopes, organization, dreams and unified hard work for food, clothing, housing, financial assistance, and jobs as if they were women--the weaker sex.

As the black woman is a constant and ever present reminder of what the black male should be, the resentment that some black males feel toward strong, ambitious black woman may periodically reach the level of hatred.

When a black male disassociates himself from the black female...it appears as if he no longer appears black. Running from his blackness and all its trials and tribulations, the disassociated black male denies his own identity, but only to himself. Thus the black male who hides, denies and runs from his true identity as a black male can never be whole to find true, maximum and ultimate happiness and success. Black males who contribute their shortcomings and weaknesses to their black skin tones, erroneously believe that deliverance can be found in the lighter flesh tones of non-blacks, particularly white women.

As black males seek out white women for serenity and tranquility, many would be surprised and appalled by the history of acceptance of black males by white women. As most social norms are rooted in historical times, so is the pampering, catering and worshipping of black males by white women.

Elizabeth Cady Stanton, a founding member of the women's rights movement and active member in the antislavery struggle along with Susan B. Anthony in 1864 stated, "*For the highest virtues of heroism, let us worship the black man at his feet.*" As some black males relish and take great pride in the acquisition of a white woman, many unwillingly sacrifice full manhood as the white women who adore them claim heroism in worshiping and petting the black male as one would pity a hurt and wounded puppy.

Thus thousands of black women must rely on their inner strengths for support, guidance and direction in most areas of their lives, including the workplace, the home and black communities. But the weakening of the black male cannot be totally blamed on white women, as the same liberation movement led black women to take aggressive roles in their interaction with black males. Since the seventies black women have freely become the aggressors in their relationships with black males. The black male, with an already fragile sense of manhood as a result of slavery, willingly surrendered much of the responsibilities in his relationships with women.

Unaware that black males would become so soft and fragile, ambitious black women out of self-reliance and maybe even loneliness become more driven and determined to succeed. Black males of the nineties reverently cling to the excuses of slavery as their reasons for their modern-day shortcomings.

The experienced black woman realizes and accepts that the forces outside herself that can assist and guide her may oppose or mislead her. BUT more importantly the smart, experienced and ambitious black woman realizes that her opposing forces can also assist her in achieving the freedom, prosperity and ultimate success that she seeks. The hopelessly, angered or passive black male refuses to abstract the good of a situation, if he cannot gain complete control and ownership, thereby overlooking and wasting the valuable resources of experience, education and awareness that lead to success.

The wise black woman does not always trust others to "do the right thing" where she is concerned. On many occasions, the black woman discovers that though she may laugh, joke and socialize with some associates, they may attempt to stand firmly as barriers between her and personal growth and or success. The smart black woman comes to realize that doing a good job or "just going along" is not always enough in striving for excellence and ultimate success. Successful people prove that one must be smart, flexible, persistent, attentive, creative, disciplined, committed, sensitive, organized and wise to pass through the final doors from mediocrity to excellence.

Realizing that life is a game that everybody wants to win, black women know that there are spoken and unspoken rules for some and hardly any rules at all for others. From experience, black women realize that some people will play by the rules, some will not. Moreover, black women realize that there may be different sets of rules for different groups of people. She realizes that one's status in life may be a determining factor relative to the rules and regulations that one is governed by. This most blacks recognize as "the system."

Disappointed and frustrated, black women come to realize that even though black males are quick to involve themselves in gaming or sport activities in all out efforts, they are least likely to put forth all out efforts in the games that matter most. Where black males will volley for the most women, jewelry, expensive clothing, or illegitimate children, the thought to enter into the games of large scale real estate, housing, banking, food supply and hotel ownership in all out efforts seems not to enter into their minds.

The harsh realities of life, rudely awakens the young, black woman with hopes, dreams, goals and a vision. With this she is transformed from a state of naivete and innocence to

womanhood. The real world has formally
introduced itself. Certain questions arise
again. Where do I fit? Where should I stand
and why? What is my destiny to be? What do I
want and how bad do I want It? What am I
willing to compromise. What am I willing to
sacrifice? What are my strengths? What are
my weaknesses?

Unfortunately for some middle class whites
they are never forced to ask and answer these
questions for themselves because they have
lived for many years with the attitude that life
will always continue to be wonderful as long as
they remain, simply white. An article in the
Detroit News on September 2, 1992, by Robert
Shepart (United Press International) entitled
"*Income Forecast Is Bleak For Men*" suggests
that regardless of one's skin color, men won't
match fathers (income). A congressional
report released findings that male workers
during the last four decades showed a pattern
of decline relative to earnings. The decline
was shown to be in the 1970s and the 1980s, for
workers in their youth, mid-life and late
careers.

The article about men's earnings said the
decline was attributed to shift of economic
tides in the decades of the seventies and
eighties. The report said that if the indicated
trends continued as such, young men can
expect lower initial earnings in their 20s,
slower earnings growth in their thirties,
stagnant earnings growth in middle age, and
sharper earnings decline as older men. This
trend is proving true as all males are
beginning to suffer the consequences of
unexpected lower incomes, employed by large
corporations that cut costs, jobs and employee
benefits to remain profitable and survive.
Additionally whites are coming to realize that

169

natural disasters like tornadoes, earth quakes, hurricanes fires and even divorce is wrecking havoc on their perfect "white" worlds rendering them less fortunate, homeless or destitute.

The black woman, has always had to be concerned about a different angle or creative twist to survive and or maintain a chosen level of success. Unlike most whites, the ambitious black woman realizes early in life that she must first learn about herself before she can adequately acquire and maintain a level of success. The black woman is forced to determine for herself the characteristics of her mental and emotional makeup that brings her to a productive state of being. To survive and succeed the black woman realizes that she must continuously enhance her positive assets while eliminating the negative and worthless. The black woman striving for success is forced to *honestly* identify both her weaknesses and her strengths.

Because of the privileged status that white skin tones afford millions of the human race, whites often fall victim to the first sign of adversity or mishap in that they believed that their white skins were their safety nets, umbrellas and shields against poverty, drug abuse, unemployment and simple confusion. I am absolutely amazed at the number of 40 to 50 years old males who live entire lifetimes only to find that they have lived almost entire lifetimes with little or no fulfillment at all. When I say to them, "then do something." The reply is always the same, "I don't know what to do. This statement shows a lack of self and social awareness.

The ambitious black woman continues to be flexible and open to new ideas and change throughout their entire lives. With a basic understanding of how society functions, black women seek to discover how to best acquire and obtain the tools, knowledge and wisdom necessary for her own definition of success and happiness.

The black woman's nature, like most other women dictates that she should have whatever she wants to feel satisfied and proud as a woman, not a black woman, not a minority but a "woman." The black woman feels that she deserves to be successful, prosperous and treated with dignity and respect. From a position of inner strength, confidence and beauty, mentally and emotionally secure black women believe in their abilities to achieve living standards that are satisfying and fulfilling. Millions of males, however, both black and white succumb to the ravages of male bonding that dictates that if one's peers go along with passivity, ignorance, violence, destruction, unemployment, drug abuse and other life threatening negatives, then they too must go along. Education has failed to teach males that a perceived friendship or association with other males does not always lead to success, or even the right choices in life.

The black male seems most surprised and intimidated by the the confidence of the self-assured black woman. One of the major complaints from blacks males about black women is that they are much to opinionated. In essence black males complain because black women are known to think for themselves, thus forming their own individual opinions about themselves and life. Black males are resentful because male bonding forces them to take on the attitudes, opinions and beliefs of their peers, thus giving up their rights to think for themselves, as individuals.

Black males influenced and imprisoned by male bonding and peer pressure, is most evidenced when in one-on-one interaction with one black male, his demeanor, tone of voice, physical presentation is normal, cordial and congenial. But in the presence of other black males he is forced to take on a "cool," "aloof," "condescending" and "cold-hearted" presence.

Black males complain that they are alienated, separated and isolated from main stream society because they are misunderstood by mainstream society. Black males are alienated, separated and isolated from prosperity and success because many do not have the courage to stand behind their beliefs, values and morals for fear of not being accepted or viewed as cool or super macho by other black males.

Black males, like many whites are distancing themselves more and more from realizing American dreams because they are not adequately dealing with their weaknesses in an effort to realize their individual strengths. Black males, like generations of frustrated whites are not dealing with their weaknesses because they feel they have no personal weaknesses, based on their racist or sexist attitudes and beliefs. Troubled and frustrated blacks and whites point to factors outside themselves as the main reasons behind unemployment, disappointment, hopelessness and despair...a typical excuse, "it's the government's fault."

Non-blacks are surprised to find that black woman are proud of who they are and where they come from. From personal experience, whites with subtle racist attitudes are

172

surprised to find that all functional blacks are not ashamed of being descendants of slaves from Africa. Whites seem also surprised that not all mainstreamed functional blacks strive to disassociate themselves from their African ties or backgrounds and that black history is not a source of embarrassment and shame.

Whites often appear surprised by the lack of embarrassment by some black women at the mention of African or African American ties. Whites are surprised, no doubt because of the functional blacks who think they must act white, talk white, effecting no resemblance to their African backgrounds as they pretend to be white in order to achieve acceptance from whites. Since a vast majority of whites are reluctant to do away with their superiority complexes, regardless how subtle, they often eventually find some way to interject a derogatory racial comment in remembrance of slavery, segregation or black oppression. Often whites use the subject of slavery, Africa, segregation or discrimination as a means to dampen the spirits of an over-confident black person. However for a black person who is aware and proud of one's past and present status as a black person of African descent, whites will come to realize that it is their own insecurities that prompts the use of the pains of black history in America as weapons against blacks in casual conversation as a means to gain or maintain an edge.

In American society, competition has become a normal factor of human nature among most people and activity. And since the diminishing of American dreams, competition has become so prevalent in American lifestyles that competition has aided in the destruction of American values, morals, families and dreams. So strong is the desire to be happy and feel good about one's self, that some Americans excel in violence, drug trade/abuse and violent crimes to satisfy their human needs and desires, never mind that their behaviors are destructive to themselves and others.

In retrospect, the harmful effects of the actions and behaviors of criminals often goes without remorse as criminals are fulfilled by the sense of empowerment and achievement that crimes provide for them. And with the vast number of people overwhelmed by substance abuse, self-destructive individuals trade reality for momentary bouts of false and illusive happiness.

But in our over-zealous quests, for success some aggressive, ambitious Americans have pushed others completely out of the game. Not that aggressive ambition is negative, because it is not. But as the hopes and possibility of American dreams continue to die it is necessary for all of us to re-establish values, morals, attitudes and behaviors and activities that contribute to the survival of America, American dreams, as well as the betterment of the entire human race.

Luckily, there *are* people who feel good enough about themselves to appreciate and compliment the achievements of others. On the other hand there are some of us who find it absolutely impossible to compliment or acknowledge another person's success or achievement. Though most of us present ourselves with great confidence and arrogance, our insecurities become obvious when we cannot allow ourselves to compliment or congratulate others when the opportunities arise.

Personal insecurities make us feel uneasy, envious and resentful of the accomplishments of others, regardless how small. It seems that many of us conclude that if we encourage by compliment, we will give others the added confidence and validation necessary to become better human beings. Most of us do not realize that in withholding the complimentary push that all humans require to feel good and grow, we stifle and stagnate the overall process of human development and survival.

It is inevitable that all of us constantly weigh and measure ourselves, our achievements, our looks, our status against others. Thus it cannot be avoided that most of us will at some point in our lives be forced to realize that someone else is prettier, more handsome, stronger, more disciplined, luckier, faster, more committed, richer, more intelligent and more persistent. People with healthy attitudes are able to accept the qualities of others. People with unhealthy attitudes and strong insecurities, are unable to accept the value and quality of others sometimes to the point of self-destruction or the attempted destruction of others.

Life has many systematic and institutionalized obstacles and hurdles regardless of ones race, sex or socioeconomic background such as the educational processes, governmental rules and regulations (laws), taxes, etc. With these in mind, some of us become very resentful when a common, ordinary human being poses as a threat to our well being or the *greatness* that we have established in our minds about ourselves warranted or unwarranted.

Most people in America, are no doubt most surprised, shaken and taken aback when it is a black woman who makes one question one's self-worth, value, intelligence, beauty and overall potential for success. A black woman who presents herself as intelligent, strong, accomplished and successful is most reluctantly accepted because [erroneously] in the minds of most Americas, white men rate highest on most human value scales, with white women after them, black males are rated next to last with black women below them. It is wrong to judge a person on the basis of race, sex, age or nation of origin.

The sense of wonder and surprise about the black woman is evident, even in the twentieth century as most people have not been properly educated to realize that the black woman has, does and will always continue to contribute to the betterment and survival of herself and mankind. The accomplishments and achievements and goals of the black woman are not always willingly accepted even among blacks. But as black women continue to contribute to the survival of mankind, they will always aid in destroying the racism, sexism, insecurity and discrimination that stifles the growth and survival of the human race.

Because some of us have such strong personal insecurities, resentment and envy may cause us to display or even act out hostile behaviors and actions. An insecure envious or jealous person usually sets out to discredit, degrade or even destroy those who appear more valuable, more accomplished or bound for success. Because a black female is least expected to display signs of value and great worth, insecure individuals readily set out to make her feel small, smaller and smallest among others.

The process of dealing with the insecurities of others can start very early in life for the black female. As millions of black females and males as well, are raised in environments of poverty, single-parent homes, drugs and other adverse conditions, young black children destroy the hopes and dreams of one another as they violently strive to impose upon other children the pain and suffering that they experience on a daily basis in the home and in their communities.

Education has failed to teach Americans how to adequately deal with pain, suffering and violation. Because millions of people have been conditioned to ignore and hide weaknesses, many of us set out to transfer our pain, suffering and violations on to those viewed more vulnerable than ourselves. The compelling twist to the human transfer of pain and suffering is often discovered that those who pretend to be most strong, accomplished and superior are most often those most insecure, emotionally fragile and most doubtful of their self-worth and potential. Experienced and smart black women come to realize that expressions of envy and resentment (from others) is often a compliment turned inside out.

The black woman in America may feel that others try to make her feel inferior and unwelcome because of her skin tone that may range from caramel to black. This confuses the black woman. The socially aware black woman reasons that all over the world "chocolate" is a favored flavor among millions. Moreover, chocolate is often "the" preferred flavor for most non-blacks. The black woman wonders. "If non-blacks really dislike me because of the color of my skin how can they (non-blacks) stand to "eat", to taste, to totally consume a food so much like me and proclaim it's scrumptiously, irresistible taste even to the point of addiction. Think about it? The black woman knows that she is of the same unique and precious quality as the world's finest and most exquisite chocolate...you can't help but love it or her. But of course, with most addictions, there is always denial.

The black woman longs to establish, display and present her finest qualities to mankind and society without prejudice. It is not the desire of the black woman to make others feel inferior, intimidated or threatened. It is, however the desire of the black woman to display her beauty as a person to enhance the beauty and value of others. Without full acceptance and contribution of the black Woman the entire human race misses out on key elements essential to maximum social growth, intellectually, spiritually and in all other aspects of life.

In order to get beyond the ravages of poverty, unemployment, violent crime, hopelessness and despair, we must all ask ourselves why we find it necessary to stand as barriers between the black woman, growth and success. Are we afraid that the black woman may actually be as intelligent, strong and beautiful as we secretly believe her to be? What is it that forces us to separate, stifle, restrict and confine the full beauty, intelligence and strength of the black woman?

Once America realizes, admits and rids itself of the forces, attitudes and actions that maintain the alienation, separation and oppression of the black woman, America will once again regain the knowledge to restore American dreams. The black woman of the nineties is ready to present her worth and value because she has emerged as a black woman more beautiful, intelligent and worldly that ever before. The black woman of the nineties has reaped the benefits of battles fought for more freedom; freedom to be all that she was meant to be...freedom to love, live, explore and contribute to the survival of mankind.

The black woman/female of the nineties has available to her every single aspect of living that exists. Like never before, she is exposed to politics, education, finance, entertainment, sports and communication from both foreign and domestic perspectives. Global exposure is made available to the black woman through television, radio, magazines, books and newspapers. The most intricate and intimate details of all significant events are available if she is interested. Without formal education, it is possible for the black woman to obtain knowledge about almost any given subject known to man, even to the point of becoming an expert.

Thousands of black women have become quite enterprising, taking their interests, pleasures and talents a step beyond what is expected, anticipated or even imagined. Successful black women of the nineties have come to realize that great rewards are available to those who have the courage to reach for the highest heights--relative to one's own pursuit of happiness. Moreover, ambitious black women have rid themselves of the negative baggage and peer pressure that holds most blacks below the poverty lines, oppressed by their beliefs that they are inferior and undeserving of the best.

Black women with self-assured, healthy, honest attitudes realize that they do not always have to reach for the highest of heights. However the successful black woman of the nineties and beyond has proven and will

continue to prove that in reaching just a little
higher everyday, every month, every year she
continues to rise upward toward heights
higher than she ever imagined. With the on-
going process of reaching, stretching and
striving the black woman goes forward and
upward, growing stronger in many ways. By
contrast, the black male has not yet fully
accepted the fact that he must adjust his
behavior and thinking to that of future growth
and positive possibilities if he plans to
establish and maintain satisfying life
standards.

The black woman feels good about her
progress. And though she has every right to
feel good about her accomplishments, society
often forces her to hide her success and
achievements for fear of negative retaliation
by those who hold authority or power over her.
In the workplace whites openly discuss their
boats, cottages and other luxuries. But
according to blacks who have been in the
workforce for more than fifteen years it seems
to be the norm or common practice that blacks
should hide the fact that blacks also are able to
afford some of the finer things in life. From a
personal experience, an immediate white male
supervisor once questioned me about the
amount that I paid on a monthly basis for my
apartment. Caught off guard, I told him the
truth about my monthly rental payments and
from that point on my hours were cut...which
resulted in a drastic reduction in pay. To this I
can only say that:

*If I knew, without a doubt, that I were superior
to someone, it would not bother me to see that
person do well for themselves. Further, if I
knew with the assuredness that whites have
established, that I was superior to all others, I
certainly would not feel compelled to use my*

180

authority to unjustifiably detract from another person's well being out of resentment on my part. And further if I knew that I was superior to all others, but became somewhat threatened by the progress of another, I would be strong enough to enhance my own strength by work, education and growth and not by snatching the rug out from under the feet of one known, established and maintained as vulnerable, simply because I have the power or authority to do so.

But not only must the black woman hide her accomplishments from a white, male dominated workforce, she must also hide her intelligence from the males that she may desire to date as a pastime or for whatever reason. In 1992, when there is obviously a problem between black women and black males, I have been instructed for the last year by black men (old, young, single and married) to hide my intelligence, my ambition, my imagination, my strength, my hopes, my dreams and even my computer from males if I wish not to intimidate and frighten them away. *This is a sad commentary about black males who liken themselves to men.*

The black woman sensitive to most of the trials and tribulations that she may encounter, appreciates every obstacle or a hurdle removed. With each new stride, the black woman knows how far she has come and how far she has yet to go to reach her maximum potential. Deep inside a black woman is a pride that sometimes rages as strong as any stormy sea. Thus, the pride alone, of a black woman can bring much sorrow, misery and pain as she continues her struggle to survive and prosper...with or without a black man by her side. Few can understand the pain of a black woman.

But through it all the black woman still looks up and around at much trouble, grief and strife with concern and compassion in her heart. The black woman, not one to die of self-pity desires to improve upon life for herself and others regardless of race, age creed, color or plight because of her past and present kinship with pain, sorrow and suffering...the black woman, the mother of all, no doubt has the answer to our troubles and our woes.

The black woman of the nineties, like those before her, is caring and compassionate, though hurried she may be in spirit. She is strong but in a very different way from her sisters of slavery and struggle. Subconsciously, unable to forget the ties to Africa and slavery, some black females are growing up confused, lost, frustrated and angry. Society is failing the young black female, society is failing itself. Because of the overall educational deficiencies in America young black females do not know where they stood in American and world history. Hence young black females do not not fully understand what they must do to aid in the survival of mankind and without the black woman, mankind cannot and will not survive as it can and should.

Even to the black woman herself, she is a mystery untold. Deep inside the black woman of the nineties and beyond, is an undiscovered, undeveloped, untapped, phenomenon. Intimidated fear may keep it locked inside forever, as America struggles to heal its bleeding wounds of self-defeat, depression, oppression and destruction.

The accomplished, black woman of the nineties, is determined to succeed against all odds. Because of her independence and newfound financial stability, she is confident about herself and her abilities to do whatever she feels she must in life to feel happy and proud of herself as a black woman. The educated black woman, true to herself, to others and the black race knows where she has been, where she is and she knows where she wants to go. The confident and socially connected black woman knows that if she continues, steadfastedly on her journey to her chosen destination, she is bound to arrive without fail.

Even a *basically* intelligent black woman realizes that education is an essential and vital key to acquiring success. A black woman who is socially aware also realizes that formal higher education is not the only avenues and pathways to success. A black woman, eager for a role model need only go to a local library to find scores of individuals who achieved great success, against great odds, adversity, pain *and* suffering.

In that there has always been an air of distinct "class" about the black woman, the black woman of the nineties is usually well groomed, refined, polished, poised, while some black women have become somewhat snobbish and arrogant as a result of their achievements and accomplishments. Some of them have even taken on the personas of black males who wear $400 suits with no money in their pockets. Like the black males, they lie to no one but themselves.

The black female of the nineties that society labels as dysfunctional, unemployable or a failure is the black female that may have been born into a family of extreme poverty. The troubled or socially disconnected black female of the nineties is the black female who may have been born into a home and community

183

environment of violence, drugs, abuse, illiteracy and all the other ills that prey upon vulnerable black families and communities.

The black female that is drug addicted, illiterate or rendered, socially null and void is a black female that is most likely a victim of a society that turned on itself. A society that turns on itself is a society that establishes and maintains drug abuse, illiteracy, poverty, welfare, unemployment, racism, discrimination, single-parent families, physical and sexual abuse and a loss of hope among it's people. In that America is a country that has turned on itself, America turns on vulnerable young people, regardless of race creating the dysfunctional, individuals who harm themselves and others.

And as America becomes number one in social ills (compared to some countries) weakening its ability to survive and grow, America is inevitably creating and rendering people who are unable to function, grow and survive. And if either is to recover, America and ALL its people, the two must work, simultaneously, hand and hand together, to heal the life threatening wounds that infect each and every American with frustration, anger and pain.

Though I feel a great sense of regret and sympathy for any frustrated, disconnected and socially dysfunctional individual, particularly, black females, I must adamantly state that no one in America should live a life that is less than satisfying. But more importantly, anyone who wants a better life must be willing to work hard and smart, while facing all odds and obstacles, in defense of one's right to have equal access to all the splendor, luxuries, riches and beauty that life, has to offer.

However, I make no excuse or feel no sympathy for the healthy, physically fit, socially dysfunctional and disconnected person who spends an entire lifetime drenched in hopelessness, self-pity, despair, anger and defeat. If Americans are to revive their hopes, dreams and possibilities for prosperity, each and every American must individually believe in his or her own rights to be successful while working collectively along with all other Americans to revive American dreams of prosperity, equal opportunity and peaceful living.

But as blacks are beset with the greatest amount of challenges and obstacles in America, blacks must first of all believe and convince themselves that they are deserving of quality living standards and lifestyles. Because in as much as blacks loudly proclaim that they are deserving of equal rights because they were born equally created to all mankind, a vast majority of blacks truly believe that they are undeserving of equal rights and opportunities. And judging from the behavior or many blacks, some blacks keep themselves oppressed as they appear to believe and maintain the fallacy that they are an inferior people simply because they are black.

The theory that it is possible for one to become in life whatever one desires, regardless of race or sex through hard work and determination has become nothing more than a worn out cliche' for a vast majority of blacks uneducated, as well as educated. Afforded basic freedoms like the right to eat at any restaurant, to study at any school, to shop at any store and be treated with dignity and respect, a vast majority of blacks no longer strive for higher heights in the areas of business ownership, greater economic power,

185

greater economic strength and greater contributions for the betterment of mankind. Too many blacks feel that they have "made it" once they are on a job for five years. Blacks quickly site the challenges that they face as the reasons behind their passive attitudes toward increased economic strength, stability and power for the black race which would in turn aid in the survival of America.

The challenges that blacks face in acquiring the economic strength and power that would aid in healing many wounds of poverty, unemployment, substandard housing and ignorance amount to countless phone calls, applications, conversations, organization, planning, commitment, tenacity, discipline, teamwork and consistency in building businesses.

Blacks would not continue to oppress themselves in poverty and ignorance if they were properly educated to appreciate the challenges of their black ancestors of slavery as they were subjected to grueling and cruel physical labor--real challenges. If blacks felt the black pride that they claim to feel, blacks would force themselves to make those extra telephone calls, take those extra classes and go beyond the last rejection if they thought back to their black ancestors who were beaten sometimes to death, if they stopped to take just one breath after countless hours of farming in the production of rice, sugar, cotton and tobacco for more than 200 years from the 1600's until the 1860s for no pay or gratification at all.

And blacks could not speak of challenges if they were properly educated to appreciate the pain and suffering of their black ancestors who produced the wealth on which the growth

of America was built. And after slaving to
build what they could not enjoy, blacks
continued to strive for freedom as when
Harriet Tubman in 1849, traveled 90 miles on
foot through swamp and woodland, alone to
gain her freedom from slavery.

For modern day blacks to speak of challenges
as obstacles, is a slap in the face of blacks who
died for the privileges, freedoms and
opportunities that blacks in America now
enjoy. For blacks to speak of challenges is to
insult the struggle and death of Dr. Martin
Luther King Jr. in his fight for the civil rights
of the oppressed regardless of race. For blacks
to speak of challenges, is a sign of their
ignorance in not realizing that though the
roads have been paved for their freedom and
opportunities, they must be patched and
repaved just like the highways and byways we
use in our day to day travels of our own free
will.

For blacks to site *challenges* as their feeble
excuses for not starting business they have
forgotten their kinship with blacks of Somalia
who in 1993 will die by the millions from
starvation, as they wait for [no doubt] whites to
aid in their rescue of which blacks in America
should share in. Blacks also must realize that
it is our fault that thousands of Haitians must
die on the waters or be sent back to Haiti to die
because blacks have NOTHING to offer these
black people in refuge against starvation,
violence, persecution and death.

As blacks continue to complain of the obstacles
in America in contributing to the betterment
of mankind, a hunger ravaged woman and
child of Somalia will challenge themselves to a
130 mile walk for food amid rotting corpses

along the journey of those who simply dropped dead of starvation.

For anyone, particularly blacks who might want to assist Somalia refugees in Kenya or elsewhere, listed below are world aid agencies based in the United States and Europe to ensure receipt. The information was taken from a special section of the Detroit Free Press on Wednesday, September 16, 1992 entitled "Quietly, A Nation Starves. *"Without Food the Body Slowly Destroys Itself" by Bill Laitner, a Free Pres Health Writer*

Care International, 660 First Avenue, New York, NY, 10016; phone 1-800-521-CARE (anytime); raises funds to distribute food in Somalia.
American Red Cross, Box 37243, Washington, D.C. 20013; phone -800-842-2200 (anytime) raises money for a variety of Somalia-related projects.
Doctors Without Borders USA, 30 Rockefeller Plaza, Suite 5425, New York, NY 10112; phone 1-212-649-5961 (9-5, Mon-Fri.).
World Concern, Box 33000, Seattle, Washington, 98133; phone1-206-546-720 (8-5, Pacific Time, Mon.-Fri.), or for recorded information anytime phone 1-800-832-6463; operates feeding centers;
Save the Children Fund, 54 Wilton Road, Westport, Conn. 06880; phone 1-800-221-2200 (anytime); feeds children; does not handle adoptions.
USA for the UN Hight Commissioner for Refugees, 2012 Massachusetts Ave. NW, Suite 500, Washington, D.C. 20036; phone 1-800-220-1115 (9-5, Mon.-Fri.); indicate correspondence and donations for Somalian assistance.
UNICEF, 33 East 38 St., New York, NY 10016; phone 1-212-686-5522 (9-5, Mon.-Fri.)

responsible for refugees; does not handle
orphans.
UN World Food Program, DC-1, 1 United Nations
Plaza, New York, NY 10017; phone 1-212-963-
8439 (9-5, Mon.-Fri.); private donations are
used for nonfood items.
Africare, 440 R Street NW, Washington, D>C>
20002; phone 1-202-462-3614 (9-5, Mon.-Fri.).
Air Serv. International, Box 304, Redland, Calif.
92373; fax 1-714-793-0226; flies aid materials to
Somalia.
World Vision, Box 1131, Pasadena, Calif. 91131;
phone 1-800-423-4200 (anytime); indicate
contributions for Somalia.

So as disadvantaged individuals succumb to the
obstacles in America, one need only think of
the starving and oppressed people of Somalia
who challenge themselves to walk, barefoot
and weak, more than 100 miles for just a small
helping of rice and beans. And if blacks in
America feel the black pride they claim to
have they will come to realize that in America,
there is no such thing as an obstacle in
America, only alternate routes, that lead to
success, prosperity, happiness and peace.

Frustrated, failing blacks need only realize
that "wanting" success is half the battle.
Secondly, blacks must convince themselves
that they deserve to have successful lives.
Blacks must accept the fact that successful
living is their right as well as their
responsibility. Most importantly, blacks must
be willing to WORK toward success. Blacks
must take responsibility for what they want
out of life. Blacks must not allow themselves to
become victims of the welfare system whereby
they are presented with social crutches even
though they are not cripple. And the new
welfare haven, blacks must not conclude that,

189

"if I commit a crime, I can go to prison, wherein I am fed, clothed, kept warm and dry, living worry free and happily ever after. Prison life is a tragic waste of human talent and human excellence...a human cop out. Whites must realize that whiteness of skin does not always bring the success that you desire or deserve. Whites, just as all others must be willing to take responsibility for identifying and presenting their personal excellence that will lead them to success, prosperity, happiness and fulfillment.

But as a black females strives to attain for themselves a sense of accomplishment as well as a satisfactory lifestyle, they must always bear in mind that as of 1992 black males in particular have a great deal of difficulty in dealing with ambitious, intelligent black women who set out to fully develop themselves relative to one's talents, capabilities, hopes and dreams. Black women and men must strive to attain a level of strength and understanding that will enable them to excel and still come together as adults in friendships, partnerships and marriages.

As of 1992, it seems not just a coincidence that four, noteworthy accomplished black women, over thirty are not married. Oprah Winfrey, a highly acclaimed talk show host, Terry McMillan, a best selling author, Mae Jemison, the first black woman in space, and Anita Hill, a law professor who accused, Supreme Court nominee Clarence Thomas of sexual harassment, all achieved notoriety, fame and fortune by 1992, single and unmarried.

So while black males complain of the obstacles and challenges that oppress them in American society, black males subconsciously oppress black women, as well as the black race, by not working together. Black males send out strong messages stating that should a black woman overcome the challenges between her and success, she is simultaneously building the wall that will separate her from the black male.

The black male must realize that as long as he is unable to accept the intelligence, ambition and strength of the black woman, he is rejecting a primary factor of his own sustenance and survival. On women, Ross Perot, a self-made billionaire, among the world's richest people and 1992 presidential candidate, and founder of Electronic Data Systems, (EDS), a billion dollar business, stated that in his experience, he found women more talented than men. In my own experience, as a black woman, it is racism and the overwhelming insecurities of men that run America that leave the talent, capabilities and valuable resources of women both black and white untapped to the detriment of America and the entire human race.

Through the eyes of many blacks in America, successful living is given to some. As far as some blacks are concerned, one need only be white to be happy, prosperous, successful and worry-free. In that a white majority is usually in positions of power and authority, one might think that all whites would be trouble-free. If whites were unequivocally superior to all other races, particularly those of the black race, there would be no white illiteracy, no white unemployment, no white welfare, no white homelessness, no white drug abuse, no white prison population and definitely no white suicide.

If America is to regain her sense of power and strength to restore American dreams, America must destroy the fallacy, the maintenance and systematic social structure that whites are superior to all other races, regardless of intelligence, achievement, education, perseverance, discipline, dedication, commitment, character, values, morals and contributions to the betterment of the human race.

If it were so that whiteness of skin meant utopic living, suicide rates among whites would be less than they are for blacks. According to an article in the Detroit News, in January of 1992. A suicide gap creates a statistical analysis whereby the black suicide rate is about half that of whites. The number of suicides were based on suicides per 100,000 population.

In 1988 two point four percent (2.4%) of black females committed suicide compared to five point five percent (5.5%) of white females. For that same year, only eleven point five percent (11.5) of black males committed suicide compared to twenty one point seven percent (21.7) of white males.

In 1990, there were five million plus whites unemployed, compared to only one million blacks unemployed. The total unemployment figure for 1990 was slightly over 6 million. Thus blacks comprised roughly only a small one percent of the unemployed. Yet in casual conversation, whites always state that it is the black race that maintains the population of Americans who do not work. The unemployment figures are relative to the Labor Force Participation Rate (LFPR)--the proportion of the population that is either employed or actively seeking employment. The LFPR in 1990 was 66.6% of the U.S. population.

In 1989 there were slightly over 20 million poor white families in America, compared to slightly over 7 million poor black families. In 1989 there were slightly over 20 million whites living below the poverty level, compared to only slightly over 9 million blacks below the poverty level.

Of a one hundred thousand sampling of the U.S. population, of the 24,120 aid deaths in 1990, 16,580 of those aids attributed deaths were white. Of those same 24,120 deaths due to aids, only 7,320 were black.

These figures show that whites are no more exempt from the ills and adversities of life in America than blacks. If life in America is to improve for all it must be established and maintained that successful living is earned through hard work, determination, values, goals, fairness and morals. Blacks themselves must work to reverse the belief that blacks are doomed simply because of the color of their skins.

And though blacks experience far more hardship and oppression as a group, the imbalance in suicide statistics tipped heavily on whites, indicate that blacks have stronger tendencies to at least "carry on" through much hardship and pain. But since whites significantly surpass blacks economically, blacks must force themselves to alter their lifestyles. If blacks are to ever attain economic and social equality, blacks, as a group, must force themselves to be more productive in every single facet of their lives, i.e., in education, in business ownership, in financial savings, in daily activity and individual growth patterns. An advantage, that whites have over blacks is that they inherit and pass down estates and large sums of money. If nothing less than through insurance policies, black parents should allow their responsible adult children to get policies on their parents, so that they too can gain ready made foundations on which to build legacies, empires, multi-million dollar businesses, but above all else, better futures for generations to come for other blacks and the entire human race.

Blacks leaders send long and loud messages about equality of the races and equal rights. However, black public figures fail to effectively teach blacks about discipline, commitment, values, moral conduct, self-respect, black pride, true racial equality, self-esteem and racial loyalty. Black leaders and public speakers rarely speak of the work ethics necessary that must go hand in hand with government programs, seed money, venture capital and settlement monies if blacks want to build the type of institutions, businesses and systems that can rid blacks of the oppression that infiltrates the entire black race.

Because blacks are not properly educated about their responsibilities and capabilities, blacks (as a race) are far less willing to put forth the time, effort and commitment to build the type of lifestyles, wealth, communities and value systems necessary for them to feel "equal" as a race of people and individuals in comparison to other races in America.

A large reason behind black oppression is that blacks establish and maintain entire generations of families and communities that are totally lacking in unity, loyalty, positive growth and productivity, both racially and biologically. Unlike blacks, whites, Orientals,

Koreans, Jews, Arabs stick together in support of one another in their efforts to create and maintain economic strength, stability, power and freedom. Far too often individual blacks will trade the support of the black race for the support of just one "great white hope." Out of ignorance, blacks will forever suffer varying degrees of inferiority as long as they (blacks) continue to maintain their mental images of white supremacy.

Young blacks cannot help but be negatively affected by life in black America because blacks themselves maintain and perpetuate oppressive attitudes and actions. Blacks will continue to oppress themselves unless a significant change is brought about in the minds and hearts of blacks about themselves and other blacks.

Blacks keep themselves oppressed from the absent fathers in the home to the black teachers in black schools who present themselves in unauthoritative ways with the latest hip-hop hair styles, lavish gold jewelry, flashy or casual clothing, long stone studded, fingernails, polished with a rainbow of colors, etc. Just as educational systems push for uniforms for the children to create a disciplined and controlled educational processes, teachers, as well, need to be uniformed in conservative attire for the same reasons.

In that life among blacks is heavily structured around looking good and feeling good, the good times that many blacks often experience is simple and narrow in scope. Thus blacks find themselves on perpetual treadmills in search of false and fleeting happiness. If blacks are to raise themselves above the ruts that many dig for themselves they must center their lives around GOALS, ASPIRATION, MOTIVATION, DETERMINATION, COMMITMENT, PRIORITY, LOYALTY, GROWTH, ACTION, PRODUCTIVITY AND POSITIVE RESULTS. Blacks must establish and maintain meaningful living standards if they are to ever enjoy the level of happiness, peace and prosperity that they deserve and seek. If blacks can force themselves to cease the meaningless noise and activity for just one year and pattern their lifestyles and all activities around growth, positive productivity, education, responsibility, meaningful communication, self-respect, self-esteem, confidence, self-control, obeying the law and respect for others, there will be no reason at all for any black male or female, young or old of the nineties and beyond to live dreadful lives of hopelessness, poverty, frustration, drug addiction, anger, illiteracy, violence, oppression and despair.

The adult of the nineties that has been nowhere, is currently nowhere and plans to go nowhere lives a horrible life of mere existence because he/she has become a "victim" of their own pity, laziness, ignorance and self-defeating attitude among others who send out strong messages that it is ok and even fun to be illiterate, poor, irresponsible, unemployed, destructive and proud of self-destruction and defeat. All people must realize and teach others that irresponsibility, self-pity, laziness, drug abuse, poverty, illiteracy, unemployment and blackness are not terminal illnesses that go hand in hand. Blacks may not commit as many physical suicides as whites but they surely commit an enormous number of social suicides that establishes a population of "the living dead."

With all the opportunities available, blacks should be ashamed of the state that they have

196

allowed themselves to settle into. Blacks, as a group, as a race, fall far below most other races in terms of quality living standards. Blacks must realize that though it takes time, effort and hard work to establish one's self as responsible, disciplined, committed, goal and growth oriented, the rewards are well worth the efforts. And beyond feeling ashamed of the oppressive state that blacks have settled into, blacks must unconditionally, individually and collectively commit to making a change for the better. Through television, role models, books, magazines, lectures and open communication, blacks must challenges themselves and one another to lift themselves up and out of the oppressive ruts that they have leisurely settled into.

With television, books, magazines, and a society that is "open" to the public there is absolutely no reason for a black person or anyone to live an entire lifetime of illiteracy, poverty, drug abuse, frustration and unemployment. In the United States, freedom is so flexible that anyone can encounter someone in the course of a day that is willing to provide a word of encouragement, direction or advice in achieving a successful way of life...if it is sought and or accepted.

Blacks must banish from their vocabularies the word "obstacle." Blacks, must condition themselves to believe and function by a creed that "there is no such thing as an obstacle, only alternate routes." If Ross Perot, a self-made billionaire, can come to the conclusion that there are some people on welfare that are more talented and brighter than himself, poverty stricken individuals, regardless of race must realize that with a chance they can put themselves in the same position as a billionaire and 1992, presidential candidate.

197

Ross Perot, stated as the difference between himself and the poor that he encountered, was that *he got the break and they did not*. The millions of blacks that find themselves isolated and separated from mainstream society and success must realize that they are not alone in their pain, frustration and struggle to survive prosper and grow. Blacks, however must realize that they themselves might have to create or seek out the break that may provide an escape from oppression in America.

As a black person, I know that "the break" that can make or break an individual comes in and out of the black community everyday. But because poverty, is no longer an altogether state of deprivation and despair, poor people miss their chances in life as they party in passive acceptance of poverty and oppression. In America, oppression does not always mean depression for those who condition themselves to happily accept poverty and deprivation. Thus minimum wage blacks and some welfare recipients create hard shells of false pride and arrogance that forces them to turn up their noses at other blacks who could very well be their saving grace from baseline living to meaningful and satisfying living standards, perhaps even wealth, fame, fortune, notoriety and major contributions to the betterment of their own lifestyles and the human race.

The black person, or anyone of the nineties that finds him or herself at a poverty level,below or slightly above, need only be willing to "work" at elevating one's attitudes, thoughts and actions to that of a more positive plane. The black person that finds him or herself, living below quality living standards need only be willing to work at *believing* that life can and will be satisfying, comfortable and meaningful through positive thought, effort and action. With all thoughts on improvement, growth, progress, happiness, peace of mind and prosperity, one need only, increase one's sense of concentration, commitment, discipline, responsibility and dedication toward achieving whatever is desired out of life.

As a black woman, it is quite evident that blacks have created deficiencies in themselves relative to their ability to commit and discipline themselves in setting and reaching goals. To initiate a basic effort to improve the plight of the entire black race, blacks need only address the issue of "time," for starters. Blacks are so accepting of their lack of commitment and responsibility to time that they coined the phrase "colored people's time or "CP Time." "Colored People's Time" means that being one to two hours late is still considered "on time" or "on schedule" as far as blacks are concerned. Thus blacks waste hours, days, weeks, months and years waiting for themselves and other blacks...which is ridiculous. Blacks must individually commit to being on time for work, play, dates, appointments, themselves and all other time related activity to bring about positive changes for the entire black race. Blacks must create, maintain and insist upon a collective sense of responsibility, respect, discipline and commitment toward improving the plight of the black race on a minute to minute, day to day and on going basis.

With all the mass media coverage of the ills that plague blacks in America, it is unnecessary to further elaborate on the ongoing destruction of the black race. It is important, however, that blacks in America unanimously, individually and collectively stand up to the challenge of working to end the

199

rampant, self-inflicted poverty, illiteracy, unemployment, drug abuse, black on black crime, unwed-motherhood, teenage pregnancies and black complacency that contributes to the oppression of blacks in America.

Blacks, or anyone who has the slightest desire to improve an attitude, lifestyle, living standard or ability to set and reach goals level can do so if they use this book as a symbol of achievement by a person, poor, but rich in desire, uneducated, but eager to learn, quiet with a loud inner-voice, physically weak, but spiritually strong...black and beautiful.

Just like me, there are millions of blacks and non-blacks as well, male and female all across America who fight within themselves to acknowledge and grasp the strength and courage that lies deep inside, to pull themselves out of the oppressive ruts of poverty, unemployment, procrastination, irresponsibility, frustration, depression and self-destruction. With the year 2000 on the way most anyone, regardless of race, creed, color or sex can and will be successful through consistent, on-going positive, productive thoughts and actions.

And just as millions of individuals fight and struggle for the courage, discipline, dedication, stamina, commitment, skill and perseverance to survive, prosper and grow, institutions, families, communities, corporations, companies large and small also struggle for survival. And in like fashion, America, its institutions and it's people will continue to experience hardships and despair unless all realize, accept and adopt undisputable desires and efforts toward survival, prosperity, happiness, peace and success.

It is important to forewarn black females of the added burdens of womanhood as they actively contribute to the betterment of the black race and the human race. As black women struggle for survival, they must also struggle to bridge the gap between black males and females, black men and women and same sex individuals because in the growing separateness, blacks can never expect to survive.

In that black women may more readily (than black males) accept and stand up to the challenges of personal, and racial growth for the betterment of the entire human race, black females/women may have to establish themselves as role models, mothers teachers and leaders willing to lead the way to peace, happiness, prosperity, harmonious relationships, satisfying living standards forging the way for the successful survival of the black and human race through, open-communication, on-going education, fairness, self-respect, self and social awareness, confidence, self-control, positive thinking, personal and social values, morals, discipline, diligence and daily renewing commitments to restore, re-establish, present and nurture human excellence in all mankind.

It is the black woman's responsibility to uncover and present the untapped talents, capabilities and ambitions of the oppressed, alienated and separated because it is through her and others like her that mankind will survive. Mankind will find the missing links in its survival in the black woman and others like her because she is brimming over with untapped talent and intelligence that has too long been suppressed and overlooked.

Because of the separation of the black woman from the black man and society at large, the ills that plague the black Race, continue to increase year after year becoming more and more tragic. Contrary to what non-whites want to believe, the tragedies in the cities of America are not black problems, though blacks may suffer the greatest amount of deprivation and devastation. As stated in an article of the Detroit News on January 10, 1992 by Bill Johnson in the Editorial Notebook it states that a report of the District of Columbia police found that, in 1986, twenty-one percent (21%) of the people arrested on homicide charges were under twenty (20) years old. In 1990 that figure grew to forty-eight percent (48%).

Violence is a problem of which all Americans must share in the blame. Violence is a problem, that all Americans must share in eliminating, because violence in America has become an equal opportunity offender against the rich, poor, black, white, old and young. Violence exists because Americans no longer take full responsibility for raising children who grow up with morals, values and ethics that should define one's self-respect as well as one's respect for others, the law, property, equality, institutions, justice, and the successful survival of mankind.

In 1992, as America experiences trouble in terms of losing overall strength as a nation, the leaders and pillars of tomorrow are being raised to be failures, quitters, cheaters, liars, thieves, drug dealers and violent crime offenders. And who is to blame? The mothers, fathers, brothers, sisters, neighbors, friends, associates teachers, civic leaders, government officials, media moguls and all other American citizens, who are not actively involved in at least one activity that promotes, teaches or organizes systems or programs to rid America of illiteracy, drug abuse, violence, unemployment, ignorance, racism, disease, homelessness, ignorance, unplanned pregnancy, poverty, discrimination and divorce.

If the leaders of the nineties experience difficulty in decreasing the overall decline of life in America, what is to become of America left in the hands of troubled and traumatized American children--tomorrow's adults? America is destined to fail if it continues on the pathways of poverty, illiteracy, drug abuse, disease, racism, unemployment and self-destruction. The lines of communication in America must be opened wide between all people regardless of race, creed, sex or age if America is to survive for itself, the world and mankind.

Since blacks suffer the greatest degree of oppression, alienation, deprivation and humiliation, all over the world, blacks of all ages must discuss issues that are of life sustaining purpose such as employment, education, self-respect, personal growth, positive productivity, social awareness, political involvement and contributing to the betterment of the black race and the entire human race. Thus, black males must cease their endless, meaningless conversations about partying and recreational activity. Black women must cease their endless conversation and worry over black males who have no respect for their own lives, who in turn can have no respect for anyone else's hope, dreams and overall well being. Black males and females must discuss ways to bridge the gaps within the black race that perpetuate and maintain black oppression for black children and future black generations.

Blacks must turn their conversations to the ways and means of establishing values and morals relative to behavior and conduct toward themselves and others. Blacks must discuss ways of re-establishing respect for one another, between husbands and wives, parents and children, among family members, among close friends, among associates and strangers. Blacks must discuss ways of developing a sense of love, pride, loyalty and unity among blacks that is essential in creating black environments that will serve to end poverty, unemployment and black on black crime. Blacks must discuss ways of establishing and running businesses in America to actively contribute to the workforce and the mechanics of "keeping America strong.

Blacks must discuss an action to stop black on black destruction. Blacks must discuss an across the board commitment to clean up and keep clean their communities and homes. Blacks must discuss a commitment to discipline to eliminate the word ghetto as associated with the black race. Blacks must realize that though funds may be low, city and community environments can still be clean, orderly and comfortable to promote personal growth and improved living standards.

Blacks must discuss issues concerning ways to establish a sense of commitment, work ethics, discipline, diligence, enthusiasm, dignity, honesty, integrity, unity, loyalty, fortitude, self-esteem and pride that can one day lead to a much better world for blacks and others regardless of race, creed, color, sex, age or nation of origin.

Blacks must discuss a movement to accept responsibility for the oppression that blacks cause themselves, while working to eliminate black inflicted, oppression, poverty, unemployment, drug abuse, crime, child abuse, spousal abuse, racism, discrimination, alienation and everything else that blacks do to other blacks to cause anger, frustration, destruction, deprivation and death.

Blacks must discuss their inferiority complexes that help maintain white superiority. Non-blacks, particularly whites, must discuss their insecurity complexes that lead them to oppress, alienate and separate those who must contribute to America, particularly blacks, if America is to survive.

Black leaders must discuss ways to incorporate the needs, frustrations and anger of common blacks in their agendas, so that they can affect changes that are vital to ending racism, black on black crime, black on black hate, racial, discrimination, poverty, unemployment, illiteracy and restoring American dreams.

Mothers and fathers (of all races) must discuss the issues that lead to and cause divorces, thus the broken homes that establish broken hopes and dreams in the children and adults of America. Mothers and fathers must discuss their frustrations and shortcomings as parents that cause them to raise children that are socially dysfunctional, destructive, angry and counter-productive to successful living standards in America and the rest of the world.

Young adults must discuss the consequences of their actions, i.e, illiteracy, drug abuse, unplanned parenthood and reckless delinquency. Young adults must discuss with one another the responsibilities involved with

raising children, BEFORE bringing children
into the world that they are not prepared or
capable of loving, teaching, disciplining,
guiding, protecting, feeding, clothing, housing
and raising to be law-abiding, productive
adults that contribute to the continued
betterment of the human race.

Children must discuss with their parents,
teachers, counselors, relatives, associates and
acquaintances the problems that they suffer as
children that may prohibit healthy transitions
from childhood to adulthood i.e, neglect, abuse,
exposure to alcohol and drugs, poverty,
violence, hunger, etc.

Children must openly discuss with one another
the harmful effects of peer pressure to steal, to
lie, to cheat, to destroy property, to commit
violent crimes, to experiment with drugs and
alcohol, to skip school, to disrespect one
another, to disrespect one's parents, to smoke
and to hide one's pain behind arrogance.
Children must discuss with one another how
they can work together to grow up to be
doctors, lawyers, teachers, leaders, artists,
bankers, business owners, land owners, good
mothers and fathers, presidents, mayors,
governors, congressmen/women, policemen,
firemen, legislators, nurses, and human beings
that contribute to the betterment of the human
race rather than the destruction of the human
race.

Employees must discuss with their employers
and each other the problems they face that
prohibit high level productivity in the
workplace. Employees must discuss with their
employers the problems that exist within
corporations and institutions that do not
contribute to improved living standards for
Americans and the rest of the world.

Drug dealers of America must discuss with themselves and each other ways to reorganize and turn drug trade and business into million dollar industries that contribute to the betterment of mankind rather than the destruction of mankind.

Gang members must discuss ways to stop the violence and take the same gang member population and create organizations that strive to establish businesses, such as neighborhood cleaners, grocery stores, child care centers, cultural education centers, big-brother/big-brother sister groups, talent searches and neighborhood voices that speak to politicians, corporations, banking institutions and entrepreneurs to aid in assisting the disadvantaged to mainstream and assimilate into society to promote quality living standards for all people.

Wealthy individuals should discuss ways to give back to society in order to create the opportunities that aid in the on-going establishment of intelligence, talent, excellence, prosperity, wealth, happiness and peace necessary for the survival and upward mobility of all men, women and children on earth.

National, state and local, power brokers, corporate heads, banking institutions and government officials must realize that they are significantly responsible for the fact that no longer can American living standards double every generation and a half, as was the case in the 1960's. Thus Americans that possess power and authority must discuss ways to reverse the findings of the nineties, that suggest that it would take twelve generations to see living standards double for Americans.

207

Graduate students from American schools and universities must challenge educational institutions to establish and provide students with workable skills and knowledge to function and survive in the American workforce and mainstream society in the years to come.

All American citizens, regardless of age, creed, color, sex or nation of origin must discuss with politicians on all accessible levels, the policies that need to be established to end socially systematic racism, discrimination, segregation, homelessness, oppression and the wasting of natural resources only to be found in the talents and capabilities of every single human being on the face of the earth.

There must be open, nation-wide communication among all Americans, regardless of race, creed, color or sex about the ways, means and necessary action that needs to take place to end poverty, violence, crime, racism, discrimination, unemployment, disease, illiteracy, teen-age pregnancy, child-abuse, spousal abuse, divorce, unwanted pregnancies, welfare and the overall destruction of the American dream that could one day lead to the overall demise of "America The Beautiful."

CHAPTER THREE

NEW BEGINNINGS
HOW RELATIONS, CIRCUMSTANCES
CAN CHANGE
FOR THE BETTER...FOR ALL

In 1992, the survival of America, the most
powerful country in the world, is seriously
threatened by a national debt, the loss of 2.20
million jobs between June, 1990 and January,
1992, poverty, aids, unemployment, crime and
violence. America is a country that makes
$820.23 a week--and spends $1,074.50. The
national debt of America grows $13,000 a
second. Just to keep up with the interest
payments of 1992, every man, woman and child
in America must pay $796.00 Most children are
non-wagearners and there are some men and
women who have never earned $796.00 in their
entire lifetimes and never will. Thus
Americans are unable to adequately support
government spending on social security,
medicare, civil service retirement,
unemployment compensation, military
retirement, welfare and health care benefits.

The survival of the greatest country in the
world must be saved by the concern and efforts
of every single man, woman and child in
America. Economist, Barry Bosworth, states,
"*After a decade or more in which Americans
have been unwilling to invest in their futures,
they should not be surprised that the future
looks a little grim.*" All around the world,
answers to questions old and new are being
sought. Much of what we thought is, is not and
much of what we thought will, will not. To end
the destructive cycles that dictate how we live,
learn and love, serious and drastic changes

209

must be made in the way we think, act and
work toward the future.

The world is in need of change...changes to end
the national deficit in America, hunger,
economic downturns, civil wars, poverty,
senseless killing, drug addiction and disease.
To satisfy the needs of all, we must consider an
untapped resource--the black woman. A very
important element of the human race, the
black woman in America can help heal the
wounds of civilization, as the black woman is
the mother of mankind. Thus it is the black
woman who must make the first and strongest
commitment to bring about the changes
necessary for the survival of the human race.

As all logical and rational problem solvers
realize, in order to come to any effective
solution, one must focus on the fundamental
aspects of a situation, the basics. As we seek to
find solutions to our problems, we must answer
some very serious questions. We must open
ourselves to honest and painful discussions
within families, friendships, marriages,
schools, universities, personal relationships,
workplaces, government bodies, organizations
and committees, wherever there is human
interaction. Men, women and children must
determine if they sincerely want to make
changes for the better.

Men, women and children must determine, if
they are willing to "work" for the changes to
end poverty, illiteracy, violence,
unemployment, abuse, racism, disease,
discrimination and the destruction of hopes,
dreams and quality living standards. If we are
serious about solving the problems that hurt us
all, we must stop wasting and ignoring, two of
the most valuable and talented natural
resources, known to man...children and the

black woman. As we realize that the entire
world is in a state of economic, educational and
moral decline, we all must consider very
carefully the consequences and
responsibilities of becoming new parents,
especially if we are not mentally and
financially ready.

As black women continue to cry to the
government for the increased well-being of
their children, they must realize and admit
that they themselves as mothers are mostly to
blame for the hardships of themselves and
their children. An article appearing in the
Detroit News in November of 1991 provided by
the AP and Gannett News Service out of
Washington reported that pregnancy is not
forcing women to get married.

The same article reported that black women are
giving birth to children out of wedlock at a
rate of 57 percent, compared to only 17 percent
for white women, giving birth out of wedlock.
Hispanic women account for 23 percent of the
children born out of wedlock. In the 15-17 age
bracket, 92 percent of these teenagers are
giving birth out of wedlock. Fifty-four
percent of poor children in America live in
female-headed families. These figures are
tragic, pathetic and sad. For all the problems,
we suffer, we have no one but ourselves to
blame, regardless of race, creed or color. We
must look to ourselves, individually and
collectively to solve our problems. We all must
lend a hand. Yes, the black race can complain
of less than it's "equal" share of government
and social support. However, blacks must look
to the black government officials that we elect
who fall short of what they should be doing to
secure equality for the black race in America.

Black men must move to involve themselves in effective communication with black women in commitments toward improved living standards for themselves, black women and black children. In an age where black men are most likely to fall prey to the ravages of most social ills, the successful black man becomes more and more extinct. Functional black males are more of a rarity because far too many are being born to teen mothers, out of wedlock, who are incapable of providing the type of love, support and direction necessary for the healthy upbringing of a child.

The black man and the black woman must come together in an effort to preserve, establish and develop black males who contribute to society rather than detract from it. More focus must be put on black males because black males are much more likely to become delinquent and socially dysfunctional. Young black males must strive to change the negative and derogative reputations and patterns that they have created for themselves. Black males can change the predictions that they will fail in life because they are born with valuable and precious talents, intelligence and insight. Black males waste and destroy their own lives, as a result of short-comings in the love, education, guidance and support they require to develop into responsible, law-abiding and self-respecting men. As a sad result, black males that number in the millions grow up to cost taxpayers millions of dollars in prisons, hospitals and as absent fathers. These males live almost entire lifetimes without contributing one positive thing to themselves or society.

Not only do dysfunctional black and white males, as well, waste millions of tax dollars as social liabilities, they cause a great deal of

212

sorrow and pain as a result of life threatening crimes that they commit against society. Any male capable of reading this commentary from the age of five to seventy-five should be ashamed of how the state of manhood has been degraded, devalued and almost destroyed. If the human race is to survive, all people, especially males must put forth all possible efforts to change the pathetic reputation associated with the unacceptable behavior of black males--which also now included a great number of white and other non-black males.

Young males must be taught to understand that the same energies that it takes to commit acts that are negative to society can and should be reversed to produce positive benefits to society than it's detriment. We all must take responsibility for educating ourselves and others about discipline, self-respect, positive thinking, positive productivity and purposeful living to achieve social, racial and overall human excellence.

Some bigoted or racist non-blacks might say, well, why don't we leave things as they are and go for the the total elimination of the black male, as much of society is of the idea that the poor is black and that the black race is most responsible for the decline of American excellence. The black race does not account for the majority of America's poor, but even if they were, only $1 our of every $10 is spent on government handouts, reserved exclusively for poor people. Thus poor blacks are not the primary cause behind social devastation in America.

Howard Wolpe, a Democratic Congressman from Michigan wrote an article entitled "Working Together to Renew Society" (Featured in the Detroit News on Saturday, July 11, 1992)

213

Mr. Wolpe wrote that "*we must stop thinking and talking about America's urban crisis as the problem of the poor and minorities to solve the problems of the cities is not to do something "for blacks" or for "the poor," it is to do something for all of us.*" Mr. Wolpe also stated that "*the economic and social policies that underlie today's urban crisis are threatening the lives and futures of Americans everywhere-suburbanites, no less than city dwellers, whites, no less than minorities.*" I wholeheartedly agree with the next statement that Mr. Wolpe made, "*It needs to be underscored that all Americans will suffer more and more if America's economic decline is not arrested.*" I think that Mr. Wolpe epitomized the theory of "cause and effect" as he stated, "*the degradation of some comes, ultimately at the expense of all.*"

In that blacks are very much a part of the founding, building and strength, blacks must be welcomed to participate in re-establishing the American dream. But in order to fully welcome the unconditional intelligence and talent of blacks, all Americans (including blacks) must be made aware of the contributions that blacks made to civilization.

For educational purposes, blacks invented or established the automatic car washer, the railway telegraph device, the guitar, the first blood bank in England and the United States, the brush, the automatic lubrication system, the air brake, the oil derrick, the riding saddle for horses, the fountain pen, the gas mask, the automatic gear shift, the bridle bit for horses, the traffic light, the lawn sprinkler, the starter generator, the elevator, the fire escape, the first portable X-ray machine, the directional signal for cars, the mechanical potato digger, the first clock made in America,

the telephone transmitter, the map, the beer
keg, the pencil sharpener, the ironing board,
the thermostat and temperature control system,
the lock, the lawn mower, the incandescent
lamp, the test to detect syphilis, an almanac.
(Read Ted Terry's <u>American Black History</u>,
Reference Manual.)

Further, it was a black man, <u>Lewis Howard
Latimer</u> (1848-1928) who drew the blueprints
of Alexander Graham Bell's telephone in 1876.
He taught himself to draft.   Mr. Latimer also
invented carbon filaments for the Maxim
electric incandescent lamp.   He received a
patent for it in 1881.   In 1984, he became the
only black member of the Edison Pioneers--a
small group of scientists who worked closely
with Thomas Edison.   As a draftsperson myself,
blacks still represent a small number in the
field of drafting.   Yet, blacks were
systematically barred from the field of
drafting along with women.

<u>Granville T. Woods</u>, a black man (1856-1910)
received more than 60 patents for inventions
ranging from a telephone transmitter to an
improved steam-boiler furnace.   The American
Bell Telephone Company of Boston bought the
rights to Mr. Woods telephone transmitter.

<u>Daniel H. Williams</u>, another black man (1856-
1913) was the first surgeon to open the chest
cavity and operate on a dying man's heart.   The
patient fully recovered and was released from
the hospital.   Millions of people, all over the
world benefit from this life-saving
accomplishment of "a black man."

It was a black man by the name of <u>Frederick
McKinley Jones</u> (1893-1961) who revolutionized
the food transport industry.   Mr. Jones

215

designed a small shockproof refrigeration unit for trucks. His invention made it possible for fruit, vegetables, meat and dairy products to be shipped all over the country. The manufacturing venture that he started along with his boss turned into a $3 million a year business. Their company manufactured air coolers for trains, ships and airplanes to keep food from spoiling. Every single human being on the face of the earth benefits as a result of this black man's innovative, pioneering intelligence and futuristic insight.

Moreover, it was a black man by the name of Charles Richard Drew (1904-1950) who developed a way to prepare large quantities of blood for emergency transfusions. Mr. Drew was a known authority on the subject of blood plasma. The British asked him to set up a plasma program for them. In 1942 the United States asked, Mr. Drew to set up a blood plasma program for them. Mr. Drew was appointed director of the first American Red Cross Blood Bank.

It was Garrett A. Morgan (1875-1963), a black man who received a grand prize for his invention of a "gas mask" at a New York Safety and Sanitation Fair. His mask was used by thousands of American soldiers when the U.S. entered into World War I in 1917. As Mr. Morgan was the first black man to own a car in Cleveland, being a car owner led him to come up with another invention...the three-way traffic light. General Electric Company bought the rights of the traffic light for $40,000.

Sub-humans or monkeys (as some non-blacks refer to blacks) could never have made such discoveries, accomplishments or contributions.

So even with all the negative setbacks and circumstances that the black man has caused himself or been subjected to, the black man was, is and will always be a vital element of the human race...if he does not completely destroy himself as he continues to blame non-black races for his destruction and shortcomings.

The mental and physical strength of black males all across the country is being wasted and destroyed, simply out of boredom, laziness and "learned" ignorance. This statement leads me to say that not only do black men and women fail to realize there own self-worth, but non-blacks also do not fully realize the value of the natural resource called the black man and secondly the black woman. White America and the rest of the white world blocks its own progress and full excellence as they continue to stands as walls of discrimination between blacks and their natural ability to contribute to the excellence and survival of society and the human race.

To cure the problems of discrimination against blacks, we all must recognize the damages of racism and discrimination imposed upon blacks and others who find themselves oppressed in their attempts to be positive, productive citizens of our cities, states and various countries. Blacks have heard so often that they are inferior and less than human so much, that many blacks have come to believe that they are victims of blackness. These same blacks willingly relegate themselves to a lifetime of hopelessness, despair and social pain and deprivation.

As people suffer throughout entire lifetimes in America and other countries, black men and women can do much in establishing successful lifestyles for themselves and for people of other nations if all people worked to eliminate the unnecessary fighting between the sexes and races.

But are we unselfish enough to want successful living for all of mankind?" We must ask ourselves this question before we can even begin to THINK that successful living is a possibility for everyone regardless of race, creed or color. OR has it been determined (by a small majority) that it is necessary for billions of people to live entire lifetimes in the midst of war, hunger, disease and ignorance in order to preserve a "privileged" status of living for some? But even if the answer is "yes," most people are realizing that social pain and suffering is breaking through all barriers, causing pain and destruction among all races and classes.

More and more, people are moving toward a national consensus that blacks and non-blacks alike must come together to create environments whereby every man, woman and child in America, regardless of race, creed and color can live a life that is free of hunger, poverty, violence, crime, drug addiction, illiteracy and unemployment. Before America can move forward toward social and economic excellence, Americans must work to identify and eliminate all possible roadblocks between Americans and the improved life standards they seek. If America continues to function by the same hidden agendas, America will continue to helplessly watch the greatest country in the world, destroy itself. As fifty percent of the people wage war on drugs, America can not have an equal amount fighting just as strong to keep drug traffic and trade in tact? The same is true of illiteracy, unemployment, disease, hunger, crime and war itself.

Is truth, honesty, love and peace a possibility
for the entire human race? Has it ever been?
Will we ever know? If it is really our desire to
end the rampant pain and suffering of all
nations, we must first answer these questions.
What are our real agendas? Are doctors
willing to sacrifice the reduction of the
national debt as they fight a national health
care plan to cut and control the ever rising
costs of health care in America? Are
American's getting their money's worth in
health care. America pays it's doctors more
than any of the fifteen industrialized nations,
yet American rates fifteenth in life expectancy
in 1990, number one in infant mortality (10
deaths per 1,000 live births), number one in
preschoolers not fully immunized against polio
and other diseases, number one in death of
children younger than five, number one in
reported aids cases, number one in incidences
of breast cancer and number one in medical
malpractice lawsuits.

I would like to believe that all of mankind
would want successful living for all men,
women and children. And though it may seem
that I have focused more on people of the black
race, I am aware that problems need to be
solved that impact upon all people regardless
of race. Moreover, I realize that if I am
successful in elevating the attitudes of the
black race to a higher, positive plane, the
positive effects will be felt by black and non-
blacks alike all across America.

The tax dollars that are slated to house, feed
and clothe dysfunctional black males OR non-
black males can be used to properly feed,
clothe and house impoverished children if I am
successful in providing positive motivation,
alternatives, options and energies in place of
the negative choices that too many of us make

219

in life. Americans have not effectively
stressed and established that education, open
communication, understanding and wisdom are
vital elements in creating satisfying living
standards. As blacks seem to suffer from most
social tragedies, blacks must strive to educate
themselves about great black Americans so that
historical, pioneering blacks can be used as
role models and roadmaps to future excellence
and success.

Living in a society where competition is very
intense and fierce, millions of young blacks
have been led to believe that they are inferior,
lazy, worthless and ugly. White America's
efforts and later selfish blacks have been
successful in keeping blacks divided,
frustrated and hopeless. As smart as blacks
are, they are easily and systematically fooled
into believing that they are supposed to be
victims of all that is negative and painful.
Thus millions of black children, needlessly
grow up to be inferior, lazy, worthless and
ugly adults--to themselves. Though it is
difficult to admit, a great many black adults
hate themselves and other blacks. Blacks have
not been properly educated to recognize or
appreciate their own beauty and qualities as
black people, unique in our blackness, but just
as beautiful as all other members of the human
race. Thus, blacks suffer the pains of black
hate that forces the angry black person to
destroy all that he or she represents--other
blacks.

On several occasions, in a relaxed atmosphere,
I have had black men with skin tones of the
darkest hue, see a black woman the same skin
tone (as his own) say to me that "they (black
men) do not like black women that are too
dark." To me this is an example of self-hatred
and unacceptance of one's own image.

Additionally for a black person to find another black person unacceptable, due to a black skin tone is the same racism that so many blacks have fought and died to destroy...yet blacks themselves keep racism very much alive. One man who expressed his dislike for black skin tones on women was born in Africa, but living in America. It is known that black men, yell the loudest, strongest and longest to NOT be judged by the color of their skin, yet black males are quick to judge their own counterparts (black women) by the color of their skin tones. If racism is to stop in the actions of whites, racism must first be eliminated in the hearts, minds and actions of blacks themselves.

If a black man can not find the skin tone of a black woman pleasing, this leads me to believe that he does not find his own skin tone pleasing to himself. Can the black skin tones of black males be their real source of anger and frustration? Why did Michael Jackson change his skin from black to white? Can the black male realize that as he hates the black woman and her dark black skin, he also hates himself? Thus the black male also must realize that if he subconsciously feels that he is ugly this is the way he presents himself, thus he is perceived as ugly, inside and out.

Can the black male who finds the darker skin tone of the black woman unappealing stand to look at himself in the mirror? What does he see? What does he feel? Do the black males who find dark skin tones unappealing choose non-black women (particularly white women) as mates simply because they cannot stand to look at their own image in female form? Blacks who have been willfully or unknowingly conditioned to hate their black skins are key elements in keeping the stigmas of black inferiority complexes alive and well. Because of self-hatred black males cause their own problems of racism and discrimination. Deep inside, some black males dislike themselves, thus they send out mixed messages. Black males who lack pride in themselves as members of the black race say, "respect me, accept me, hire me, love me even though I am unable to respect, accept, hire, love myself or others like me." (other blacks)

If the black male cannot respect, accept, hire and love himself, or his own kind (other blacks), how can he ever expect to be fully loved, respected and accepted among others, among other races? If the black race can not fully accept, love and embrace itself, the black race will never fully identify, establish, develop and maximize it's talents and abilities. The same is true of the white race. The white race's overly aggressive efforts to suppress and oppress other races show that it is not secure enough to welcome, recognize, appreciate the contributions and talents of races outside the white race, particularly, the black race. Thus the entire human race falls short of positive outcomes that could and should occur.

To re-establish true black excellence, blacks must stop blaming the disadvantaged plight of blacks on that of the system and its ideologies. Black men, themselves must shoulder the responsibilities for much of the pain, suffering, shortcomings, status and future of the black race. Black men and women must challenge themselves to establish and create the type of foundations necessary in creating a social safety net that will no longer allow blacks to fall through the cracks of poverty, unemployment, drug abuse, crime and self-destruction. Black men and women must begin

"today" guiding, teaching and instilling
strength in all black men, black women and
young black children the importance of
education, honesty, respect for self, respect
for others and the overall uplifting of the
black race and all other members of the human
race.

Just as America finds itself in trouble as a
world super-power, re-thinking strategies and
the way it relates to Americans and other
countries, blacks must also re-think strategies
to effectively mainstream and assimilate
within society to aid in the successful
revitalization and survival of America and
later the world. As the suffering of the black
race flows into the suffering of non-blacks
and vice versa, the lines of communication
must be opened and placed on the table to be
dealt with by all people regardless of race,
creed, sex or age.

Blacks feel it is the responsibility of "the
system" to heal its wounds. Yes, society has a
responsibility to provide equal access and
opportunity to all of life's treasures, however,
it is the responsibility of all members of the
human race to maximize one's own efforts to
block the ravages of poverty, ignorance,
illiteracy, unemployment, disease,
discrimination, abuse, harassment, oppression
and deprivation. One must initiate and develop
one's own plan and process to create and
establish life standards and lifestyles that are
comfortable and satisfying. Far too many of us
waste our lives away complaining about what
others have, yet too many of us are unwilling
to work for excellence and the greater rewards
in life.

Millions of blacks are afraid to speak up for
themselves. Black males feel that an admission

223

of pain or vulnerability caused by racism, is much better dealt with in the confines of the victims heart and mind. It is known that it is painful for black men to share their pains of racism and alienation with black women. Black women find this a great source of frustration, because black women are very much aware of the difficulties that black men face in America, because black women face the same obstacles and roadblocks. Yes, a black man's manhood rests upon his ability to provide and interact with mainstream society.

However, a black woman's womanhood also is defined along those same lines as most black women in America are forced to house, clothe and feed themselves. Thus, (so often) the class action suit. Black women are *not* able to define themselves by the quality of their interpersonal relationships as friends, mothers and sisters, as very few black women in America can rely on black men as "sole providers." Black women, are forced to accept responsibility for the way they fare in life, to the same degree as black men, i.e., education, employment, health care, housing, transportation, financial security and protection against random violence and crime.

Usually when the subject of blacks and their overall position in society arises, black males usually state, "we no longer have a leader." "We need a leader." I think to myself, is this the statement of a man or a child? I thought that it was the woman who set out to hide behind the shirt tail of a man, for protection, guidance and support. Not enough blacks are, individually, willing to take responsibility for fixing the problems that plague them personally. Blacks must educate themselves to identify their "own" problems, accept their problems, identify "various" ways to solve their problems and to solve their problems in the shortest amount of time possible. Blacks must learn to eliminate their problems so that they do not continue to run into the same brick walls of unemployment, welfare, drug abuse and criminal activity year after year throughout their entire lives. Moreover, blacks must strive to educate, young black children to prepare themselves for the responsibilities of adulthood, self-reliance, self-sufficiency, social awareness and social involvement.

Though blacks are very creative, far too many blacks have been brainwashed into living within the confines of limitations, discrimination and boundaries. Far too often, if a black person is told that there is only one loaf of bread and it is sitting on the table, the thought to look under, behind or in front of the table does not even occur. For example, blacks are supposed to be the ones with the phenomenal rhythm, yet some whites can out dance, rap and scat a significant number of blacks because whites, as a group, know no boundaries or limitations. Now some blacks, in an effort to become white, brag that they have no rhythm. Blacks have become far too passive and lazy as they enjoy small freedoms and opportunities. Blacks should be striving to achieve some of the accomplishments that whites have so long dominated, particularly in the areas of business ownership, technology and manufacturing. As many non-blacks are falling between the cracks and onto the welfare rolls and unemployment lines, blacks are not alone in becoming socially passive and irresponsible.

For instance, in going to a gas station, I encountered a young black male mechanic. The talker that I am, I asked him if he liked his

225

job as a mechanic. His reply was, yes. He goes on to add that working in a service station has it's limits in pay, benefits, growth opportunities, etc. My next question was, "has it occurred to you that the same duties and responsibilities that you perform for this gas station could be yours with a company such as General Motors, Chrysler Corporation, or Ford Motor Company?

The reply of the gas station attendant was one of surprise, "really?" I reply, if a company is in the business of making cars, the skills and knowledge of a good mechanic are extremely useful." The mechanic went on to ask how he could make contact with a large corporation, such as Ford or GM. I, replied, get on the phone and just keep calling until you get transferred to the right department--which may take ten calls or so, but just keep calling until you are told where to get an application for employment. After that don't stop calling until you get the job. But in the meantime, do research to open your own mechanic shop, just in case you never get hired. Blacks must learn to create and establish alternate routes and choices.

Proof that America's educational processes are insufficient, it never dawns on a great many blacks and non-blacks as well that if you are going to work and you have a skill or service to offer, why not work for the biggest and the best, thereby reaping the greatest amount of satisfaction, pay, opportunities and benefits. Far too many blacks reach and settle for the scraps and the crumbs at the bottom of the barrel, when opportunities are readily available for those willing to reach for the highest of heights.

Even though the job market is shrinking, with jobs lost to automation and foreign countries, too many blacks settle for employment opportunities that are too close to the cracks of unemployment and welfare. When laid off from minimum wage jobs, socially vulnerable individuals fall through social cracks to be caught by the ravages of welfare, unemploy ment, shelters, hopelessness and despair. Blacks must stop setting themselves up to fail as a result of their own lack of social and political awareness, interest and planning.

Generations of blacks, dating back to the seventies, have not been taught to effectively think, comprehend, analyze and deduct conclusions from the information they receive via, television, newspapers and general life experiences. These same generations have become passive and lazy. Blacks realize that they are not satisfied with their living standards and most have come to the conclusion that they are powerless to make positive changes. The same is true of whites. As the American living standard decreases in value for black, whites and others, Americans are not effectively using the full benefits of education and communication to maintain the great American dream for themselves and future generations.

All children must be raised and taught to live full and enriched lives that will lead to successful living in adulthood. Adults who fall short of successful living do not possess or understand the value of education, comprehension and understanding. With public schools, television, magazines, libraries, concerts, sports and the like, there is almost absolutely no reason whatsoever for any person to go through life in America destitute, illiterate or unemployed unless he or

227

she chooses to do so out of laziness and
ignorance. Through television alone one can
get lessons in almost every subject necessary
for successful living.

In flipping the channels from program to
program one is exposed to almost every
profession in the world. If people forced
themselves to listen, grasp and comprehend
the messages, there should be no problem with
communication skills, motivation, social
awareness or articulation. Americans have
become so wrapped up in "having a good time"
most have alienated themselves from basic
intelligence and thinking. Most Americans,
young and old have become so regimented in
their daily routines, that millions of
Americans function as programmed robots,
driven by habit and conditioning. Americans
have for too long separated themselves from
creativity, imagination and personal mental
growth.

As we watch the likes of Michael Jackson,
Michael Jordan, Star Search or Lifestyles of
the Rich and Famous, we should be learning
about stamina, concentration, determination,
dedication and work ethics—get the job done
best, to get PAID the most.

As we watch the news, we should be learning
about community, state and national issues.
Being the passionate, emotional people that we
are, Americans can witness tragic events or
circumstances that touch our hearts prompting
anger, frustration or sorrow. Hence, we must
realize that the circumstances that cause
painful emotions can be changed and
eliminated. The usual response is "Oh, that's
tragic" or "that's too bad." Ross Perot's advice
on starting businesses (which would add to
America's job base) is that *one should learn an*

industry, look for unmet needs and build the business around unmet needs.

As circumstances get increasingly worse, all over the world, all Americans must challenge ourselves and each other to do all that is humanly possible and necessary to eliminate the tragedies and deficiencies that exist in America. Most people do not realize the potential for notoriety, personal satisfaction and monetary gain if one is involved in the social mechanisms of "positive" change. Socially inactive people sit back and let others shoulder the full responsibilities of righting the wrongs and shortcomings of the world. People who do not get involved are the first to complain, when they have every opportunity to help set in place new laws, news rules, new regulations and new opportunities. People, who continue to separate themselves from hard work, discipline, social interest and contribution, are the people who will continue to be oppressed as victims of their own self-pity and lack of control and interest over their own well-being.

I find it appalling to hear one say there there are not enough jobs. I find it more appalling that an able-bodied person accepts the status of being unemployable. There is a lot of work to be done and if one is not brain dead or in a coma, one is employable. But one must WANT to work. We ALL must be WILLING to work our way up to higher standards of living. Americans of the nineties do not know what *real* work is all about as they complain of fatigue at the close of their nine to five, sit behind the desk, jobs.

Much of America was built and made strong as a result of the *work* performed by black slaves who received no pay at all, wrong though it

229

was. What most Americans label as work is pure pleasure by comparison. Following is an account of *work* taken from "Before the Mayflower, by Lerone, Bennett, Jr. *For most (black) slaves, life was a nightmare of drudgery. An ex-slave has said that is seemed the fields stretched from one end of the earth to the other. Men, women and children worked. Women cut down trees, dug ditches and plowed the fields. The old and the ailing worked, feeding the poultry, cleaning the yard, mending chothes and caring for the young and sick. Males and females worked the traditional hours of slavery from can see to can't see. On most plantations a horn or bell sounded about four in the morning. Thirty minutes later, field hands were expected to be out of the cabins and on their way to the fields. Field hands worked steadily with the exception of ten or fifteen minutes at noon to swallow cold bacon, not allowed to be idle until unable to see. When the moon was full, black slaves often labored until the middle of the night.*

As far too many of us complain and refuse entry or beginner level opportunities, all Americans should be making on-going strides forward and upward. Unlimited opportunities exist to acquire unlimited wealth, prosperity and successful living, if one is willing to work; Not by by the sad standards of slavery, but by modern day standards, wrought with comfort, technology and the freedom to set one's own pace and best of all to be paid and without the fear of being whipped when tired and weak. As we wonder where to begin, a small or half step toward improved life standards is better than no step at all. Stagnate, frustrated, oppressed, depressed and angry individuals, regardless of race, age, creed or sex must learn to produce results that they can measure, build on and grow from.

In too many cases, unemployment is not an
issue of being temporarily, out of work.
Extended unemployment and welfare rolls exist
for people who have given up on socially
functional living, taken a break from life, or
too lazy to work because of social crutches
called welfare. Such was the case in 1991, in
Michigan, when some ninety-thousand (90,000)
able-bodied, single persons were cut-off from
the welfare rolls. All of a sudden you had
people almost begging to take the minimum
wage jobs, that they had previously frowned
upon and outright refused. Certain welfare
recipients were *now* willing to work for any
amount of money and the duties really did not
matter, as a result of their social crutches that
were unexpectedly taken away.

With the elimination of General Assistant, the
welfare recipients become more than willing
to work. What brought about the change in
attitude? The government removed a crutch
that was unnecessary. It probably never
dawned on the social dependents that had they
tried to help themselves before the removal of
their welfare crutches they would have been
much better off. Unfortunately, some ex-
welfare recipients wound up homeless, in
shelters or on the street--males, females,
children, black and white. These people were
not properly educated in terms of values,
morals, creativity, personal strength and
pride. A primary reason behind much of the
oppression, poverty and violence in America is
due to a deficient educational system, that must
teach values, the truth, morals, ethics, self-
respect and common knowledge if America is
too remain the most powerful, land of
opportunity that it is known for.

In America and probably around the world, we
have people with extensive formal education

and degrees that fall through the cracks of poverty, unemployment, drug addiction, hopelessness. These people were also not properly educated. Teachers, administrators, policy makers and parents must be re-educated so that the educational processes and systems that we offer in America can better serve its students. Everyone is a teacher. Everyone is a student.

Educated people may memorize a lot of facts in order to get passing grades, but some never *learn* how to properly obtain and use information for everyday living. The educational system as it exists up through the nineties does not teach students how to fully comprehend and analyze common every day experiences behaviors and systems to recognize problems, solve problems, makes decisions and functions at one's maximum potential. If Americans were properly educated, all Americans would realize the beauty and strength of education and knowledge and most would be functioning at much higher levels of productivity and performance. No doubt, there are millions of Americans, regardless of age, sex and race who have not read a book in one-to-five-to-ten years. There are some Americans who you can not even *pay* to pick up a book and read it, thus there are millions of functional Americans who are brain dead relative to new information and knowledge.

Students are not taught about common sense, logic and rational. For some people these skills come naturally. The thought processes of common sense, logic and reasoning are skills that should be practiced and used in everyday life. If America revised it's educational system to teach people *how* think, Americans would be capable of tapping into their own personal resources, talents and capabilities in order to maximize the benefits of formal and informal education.

If students were properly taught about common sense, logic and rational at early ages they would come to learn the real beauty of education itself. Most people think that in order to gain knowledge, one must be formally taught, in a classroom, by a teacher, in a public or private institution. Formal education is wonderful, great and it's benefits cannot be denied, however formal education is not complete nor is it enough. If formal education were sufficient, as Americans know it, we would all fully embrace the benefits and mechanics of teaching, learning and knowledge, which is far from the case. Far too many Americans, shun, dread and fear education. Thus we have twenty-seven million American Adults who are functionally illiterate, according to Laubach Literacy International, people who cannot read to their children, understand street signs or job applications. Pathetically, it is also stated in "We're Number One" by Andrew L. Shapiro, that an additional forty million adults have a hard time reading newspapers."

It stands to reason that America is in trouble and that the American dream is dying a slow death. The problems of America is not the fault of the President's, the government, the wealthy, corrupt corporate executives or con artists. The problems of America is the fault of every single man, woman and teenager, regardless of race who does not plan and work to establish, control and maintain a satisfying life standard for one's self and all other Americans. Ross Perot, a self-made billionaire and 1992 presidential candidate states that *if Americans want to know who's to blame for the*

$4-trillion debt, "just go look in the mirror."
(United We Stand, By Ross Perot) And to lend
further credibility to the fact that the survival
of America lies in the hands of American
citizens, an African Proverb states, *the ruin of
a nation begins in the homes of its people.*
(African Proverbs, compiled by Charlotte and
Wolf Leslau)

Because so many people separate themselves
from the full advantages of learning, we all
far short in obtaining for ourselves fully
successful lives. But then, in getting back to
basics, we must ask ourselves and one another
a very important question. Do we *really* want
all Americans properly educated? OR, do we
hold back the most important tools in an effort
to preserve upperclassmanship? During the
times of slavery blacks were beaten, whipped,
maybe even killed for the illegal possession of
a book. Blacks were prohibited the
opportunity of education. With those days long
gone, it seems ridiculous and pathetic that any
American citizen would allow themselves to be
illiterate--unable and unwilling to read. On
many occasions I have met people with degrees
that can barely read. A survey in 1986
indicated that 17 to 21 million adults cannot
read; the majority is under fifty (50) years of
age.

In 1992 as the American Automobile Industry
suffers great loses, a Detroit News Article on
Monday, January 20,1992 stated that t*he
twenty-one (21) million Americans that cannot
read averages out to eight (8) percent of the
population that cannot read at the fourth-
grade level.* This statement was derived from a
1992 report in the 1992 Information Please
Almanac. This same report states that *forty
(40) percent of high school graduates cannot
read at ninth-grade level.* Illiteracy is not a

black problem. Illiteracy is a national tragedy, that needs to be dealt with on a national and individual level. We have got to encourage each other to read so that we can raise our levels of intelligence and awareness if we are to survive as a nation within the human race. If Americans continue their same patterns of illiteracy, ignorance and irresponsibility, we all can expect much of the same confusion, frustration, depression, alienation, anger, poverty and American decline that established the $4-trillion deficit that will rob all Americans of the living standards and lifestyles that all Americans want and deserve.

All of America is suffering because large percentages of the American society and workforce is functionally illiterate and ineffectively educated. I met an attorney for a major corporation that could not determine east from west in his own community. Out of respect to his manhood, I did not press the issue. From one aspect, I did him a disservice. I preserved his ignorance to preserve his manhood. A lot of men, no doubt fall victim to this disservice, particularly black males, as women turn their heads from male ignorance as a result of male dominance and intimidation. I once had a white male manager in the workforce that could not determine a "D" from a "B" in uncapitalized form. This man was Manager of a Customer Service Department of one of the largest automotive companies in America. Ignorance in America is not a black problem. Ignorance in America is a national problem, that could very well speed the demise of "America, the Beautiful" as most people around the world know it to be.

As individuals and nations continue to suffer it is time that the issues of education, personal growth, black business ownership, social participation and awareness are talked about from new and untapped perspectives. In my observations, I feel it is my responsibility to initiate *nationwide* conversations about problems that impact on the lives of all Americans, from a black woman's perspective...Cherry Scott's perspective. My main objective of this book is to address and help solve the problems of people in America. I find it extremely disturbing that in informal relationships with most black males and females, the conversations are empty, pointless and shallow. Most conversations with women usually revolve entirely around one thing--men. Most black male conversations revolve around fun, fun and more fun.

With a $4-trillion American debt, unemployment, poverty and universal stress and strife, idle chit chat is a grave disservice to one's self, one's race, America and the entire human race. Far two many people, of all races, sex and ages do not realize that they have the talents, strength and fortitude to make significant contributions and changes in their own lives that will stand to improve life for mankind, now and for many years to come.

Far too many of us allow ourselves to waste our lives, completely submerged in shallow, meaningless thinking, talking and living. I realize it is no one's *right* to impose viewpoints upon anothers. However, if we, as men and women would just briefly steer our conversations toward pertinent relative issues such as creativity, disease control, gainful employment, ending illiteracy, ending crime, productive activity, travel, voluntary education, personal growth, racial harmony, the elimination of physical abuse, ending world hunger, planned parenthood, etc. most of us would find that there is personal, mutual interest in at least one serious national, domestic or community problem. In talking about problem issues, among family, friends and casual acquaintances, all of us would find that there is enough mutual interest, concern and personal power to solve the problems that hurt all Americans a lot faster than a small group of government officials and power brokers who really do not fully understand what the problems of the American people really are.

Once Americans identify and acknowledge their mutual concerns and solutions to solve the problems that plague all Americans, we can go forward in sharing the responsibility of solving the problems that plague us and our societies. In our meaningless existences, we continue to rely on a select few, such as the government, and social servants willing to work for the causes of which *they* believe in to make, first and foremost, *their* lives better. You and I have to also work for the causes that you and I believe in to make *our* lives better.

Americans must individually take more active roles in government, education, law and health care policy making concerns. Common sense deducts that governments can not possibly save us all. Yet year after year, adults become less and less involved and interested in the vehicles of change that affect all our lives. Americans now wait until overwhelming stress and strife infect their lives before getting involved. We all must contribute in saving ourselves from the problems of ourselves and the problems of others. We must admit and realize that the problems of others can not only hurt us, but they can kill, making us all victims of the societies that we, ourselves have created.

People of the nineties find ourselves in
extremely troubled times. The early nineties is
a time where domestic and world relations have
gotten out of control, hinging on mass
destruction and social decline and decay.
National concerns continue to decline as we
continue to depend upon others to solve the
problems of America. It is ridiculous to even
think that the American dream can be restored
without the help of all American citizens
regardless of age, sex or national origins.

All presidential candidates (Bush, Clinton and
Perot) of 1992 agree that the American people
must be put back to work. However all three
failed in their campaign callings to stress to
the American people that it is the
responsibility of all American people to help
create those jobs. Knowing the mentality of a
wide cross section of young people, they are of
the mind that the jobs necessary to maintain
American strength will systematically drop
from the sky. We alone, together, must work to
re-educate, re-structure and re-empower
ourselves and our nations, if we are to survive
to experience prosperous, healthy and
satisfying living standards.

At only sixteen, young Darryl Bernstein has
the right idea about establishing and
controlling his life. Already he has headed
more than 50 small businesses, from a
lemonade stand to a graphic design company
and house-checking service. He has even
written and published his own book, "Better
Than a Lemonade Stand: Small Business Ideas
for Kids" (Beyond Words, $7.95) *Daryl's book
gives advice on how to start 52 different small
businesses. His small business ideas range
from being a baby-sitter broker to making
wake-up calls. Dary's Top Tips include: Even
though you are young, you can do great*

238

things--including running a small business--
if you put your mind to it. Watch for
opportunities. If you look, every day you can
see new ways to make money. Choose a
business you enjoy; you'll do better. When you
are starting and running your enterprise,
keep in mind that school is important. It will
help when you are older. Stay Organized. Be
on time or a little early. Be patient and don't
give up. If you keep trying, you will succeed.
When dealing which customers, be very
courteous. Be proud of your success. (Taken
from an article in the Detroit Free Press on
Friday, October 30, 1992, written by "The
Freep') The advice that Daryl Bernstein
provides is good for anyone from the ages 10 to
66, in that Daryl is an inspiration and example
of how important it is that Americans take
more responsibility for their own individual
well being, regardless of age, sex or nation of
origin.

The powers and authoritative figures that rank
highest among the American people are not
adequately aware of the needs and desires of
the people in mid and lower level statuses in
order to adequately effect positive change.
But, even if American government is basically
aware of the needs of its people, "government"
cannot possibly reach all levels, nor can it
ever adequately satisfy all classes,
socioeconomic groups and races without the
support and active involvement of all
Americans. This is not to say that government
is not sensitive to the needs of the lower or
different classes. It is only to say that WE ALL
MUST DO MORE in our efforts to save ourselves,
our children, our communities, our cities, our
states, our nations, our world. All Americans
must work to establish a work ethic that
promotes aggressive activity that produces
positive results. Many American citizens are

angry with the way the country has been run, particularly under the administration of President Reagan (term January 20, 1981 January 20, 1989) and President Bush (term Jaunuary 20, 1989 January 20, 1992).

If all Americans worked *half* as hard to express, fulfill and satisfy their hopes, potentials, dreams, talents, goals, philosophies and ideals as Presidential candidates work to get elected, America would be free of hate, illiteracy, unemployment, disease, crime, abuse and all the other ills that rob Americans of what they truly deserve in life...peace, prosperity, happiness and all around good living.

But what Americans fail to realize, is that until we all pitch in and do all that we can to improve life for all we all will continue to suffer. In the 1992, presidential campaign, all candidates, (Bush, Clinton and Perot) agree that jobs are the answer to solving the problems that exist in America. And all three adamantly proclaimed *they* would put America back to work. But what all three presidential candidates failed to impress upon the American people is that, it is the average American citizen who must establish the business, thus the jobs to put America back to work. The jobs that Americans need, to pay off the national debt, to stop welfare, to eliminate crime, to educate children, are not going to drop out of the sky. Large corporations have done all they can to put people to work. they are eliminating jobs. Many of the jobs that do exist with large corporations are constantly be eliminated due to technology, downsizing and efforts to stay in business in the nineties and beyond. So where are the jobs going to come from to put Americans to work? The American people must create jobs for themselves and others.

If all Americans do not take more active roles in their own personal well-being we can expect circumstances to get worse as we move toward the year 2000. Race, creed or socio-economic status now has no bearing on the hardship and pain that Americans suffer. Americans indiscriminately hurt each other, more and more, directly, indirectly and randomly. People are angry and they are taking out their frustrations in any way they can and on anybody they can.

In Detroit, Michigan in November of 1991, someone, from an overpass, dropped a concrete block of cement on a truck passing underneath the freeway. The boulder went through the windshield. It killed the passenger, a young white woman of thirty or so. This innocent victim was an engineer for a major automotive corporation on her way to school to further her education. She was the mother of a small child. This woman's death was a tremendous loss to her family, her friends, the workforce... the human race.

This woman was totally unsuspecting of her near death. It is very unlikely that she new her killer. Her killer probably did not know her, no doubt so disturbed that he wanted to hurt someone, anyone. The woman that died traveling under a freeway underpass could have been a high government official in a limousine. It could have been a world renown entertainer, it could have been the person to discover the cure for a deadly disease, it could have been you. It could have been me. Yet it was she who suffered the rage of the frustration of someone she never even knew.

One year later, it is suspected that the person who dropped the chunk of cement from a Detroit highway overpass, was (just as I had

suspected) a troubled and frustrated individual.
Suspected was as 13-year old boy who had seen
more than his share of violence, in his young
life. The young boy had escaped the fire of his
home that killed two of his sisters. Two years
later, he found his mother dead in bed of a
heart attack. Two years later the same boy
helped a 13-year old friend, who was killed in
the process, rob a party store. The young boy
continued to flirt with danger, up through the
overpass/concrete incident. No doubt,
overwhelmed by the unlucky circumstances, in
his life, this young man made some bad choices
very early in life.

If our family institutions and educational
systems were more effective in helping
children deal with hardship, pain and
adversity, Americans could eliminate much of
the pain that we suffer. Some people argue
that it is the responsibility of the family to
teach children about values, morals, self-
respect and respect for others. However, we
all must take responsibility for establishing,
teaching, maintaining and insisting upon
ethics to promote, peace, harmony, safety, self-
control, self-respect, respect for others, life,
liberty, freedom and justice for all...as most
are now at the mercy of all.

In Kalleen, Texas, also in 1991, a young white
male drives his truck through a restaurant
window. With a gun he randomly shoots and
kills several people having leisurely lunches.
These people were totally unsuspecting that
this was to be their last meal. Why? Because a
young male was obviously disturbed, frustrated
and angry. As newspaper articles were
featured about the Kalleen tragedy, one stated
how he was being forced to repair a fence (on
his property). The same article stated how he
may have been frustrated over an unpaid

utility bill. Women were also stated to be a possible source of his frustration.

From my own experience, in times of financial difficulties, some utility company clerks or cashiers, can be extremely insensitive, cold and harsh in allowing arrangements to pay bills. I have been given the impression that in their positions they exhibit overly powerful and hostile behavior in their capability to demand payment or hardship—no lights, no water or no telephone service. To me if these type people desire to be powerful, they should use these strong emotions in solving real problems that plague us all like illiteracy, unemployment and juvenile delinquency, rather than running the risk of pushing a stressed out, frustrated individual, over the edge in an effort to collect or rectify a problem, valued at $100 or less.

Though operators are hired to do a job, they should realize that it is not always necessary to push a person to the edge because of one's own personal inadequacies, frustrations or problems. It is not a rarity to interact with individuals employed to serve the public who come across as rude and angry. Americans who are employed to serve the public should be courteous, polite and helpful, as they are being *paid* to provide service.

Because I do not know any public service, I have never been able to voice my concerns about the rude and hostile behavior that some exhibit in servicing the public. Americans employed to serve the public should present themselves as helpful and courteous. I wonder,was it an overly aggressive utility operator or city worker regarding the fence that caused the destructive frustration of the guy who killed the people of Kalleen, Texas.

243

We will never know because this guy's frustration forced him to take his own life. Americans realize that we are sometimes *overly* rude, nasty and discourteous to one another. All Americans must check themselves in an effort to promote more harmonious relationships and interactions toward positive chance. Like Rodney King asked, "can we all get along?" If Americans can improve relations between one another, our cities, communities and families will see far less tragedy, pain, ignorance, and suffering.

Adding more tragedy to 1991, in a United States Post Office located in Royal Oak, Michigan, a young white male goes on a shooting spree after being fired from his job. If I am correct, his targets were mostly supervisors. One of the victims was released from a previous position with the Post Office because of his nasty ways as a supervisor. The next day following the shooting, a young lady in a restaurant stated that she knew people that worked at this particular office. According to some postal office employees, she said that the victims deserved, what they got. To me this was outrageous.

A significant cause of frustration, rage and tragedy in America stems from the hateful and evil behavior of authoritative figures such as supervisors, teachers, police officers and even parents. As society often wants to blame the victim, Americans must realize that they themselves viciously strike out at others, in their positions of power,as they themselves are overwhelmed with personal anger and frustration. In violent or quiet rage, Americans destroy the lives of one another, oftentimes causing irreversible damage, sorrow, pain and death on innocent victims. Americans, must control themselves.

Americans, we must confront frustration and
anger in an effort to destroy the anguish that
we all experience in life long before it
destroys us or causes us to wrongfully destroy
the lives of others.

In my opinion, not all killers, rapists and the
like are mentally deranged...born crazy.
Destructive behavior is a level that
abusive/destructive people consciously and or
subconsciously elevate to. Destructive
behavior, we have learned is often the result
of abuses that people have suffered in their
lifetimes. People that abuse themselves and or
others were never taught to cope with the
trials and tribulations in life that anyone can
suffer. It is the pain of extremely destructive
people that becomes so disturbing that
irreversible destruction, is the only way they
can escape the madness, frustration and anger
that festers in their hearts, souls and minds.
Our educational systems do not teach that there
is always a positive, workable solution to every
problem in life. We must learn and teach each
other how to better deal with problems that
may arise in anyone's life, at any
time...unexpectedly.

Through vicious acts against society and
others, destructive people lash out to cope with
an over abundance of stress, sorrow, pain,
loneliness, anger and even power. This is
wrong. As fellow human beings we must strive
to educate ourselves and each other to do a
better job of coping with real life situations,
personal problems and social problems. We
teach all sorts of technical skills, but
Americans must learn and teach survival skills
at earlier ages to increase the ability to deal
with our emotions, both good and bad.

America must re-establish a value system that promotes self-respect, respect for others, self-control, positive productivity, positive thinking, self-confidence, individual excellence, harmonious relationships, racial harmony, education, self-awareness, social awareness and measurable contributions for the betterment of man/womankind. Realizing that not all children and adults have or had the privilege of having loving and caring parents for love, support, protection, guidance, balance and direction...Americans must teach and help each other, regardless of the relationship. Americans must realize, teach, stress and nationally proclaim that violence, drug abuse, racism, sexism, discrimination, dishonesty, stealing, lying, cheating, and any type of physical abuse is wrong.

Remembering that we are all, supposedly created equal, destructive people also have hidden talents, intelligence, and capabilities that they are unable to present in conventional ways, perhaps because of negative past or present experiences that they are unable to understand and deal with. Teenagers and some young adults, never having been taught to reject the pressure of peers to engage in destructive and or unlawful activity often get caught up in circumstances that cause irreversible damage, i.e.,. prison, drug addiction, great bodily harm or alienation from mainstream society. Overly frustrated and angry individuals give up. They feel hopeless. They feel destroyed. They set out to destroy. As human nature dictates, for almost all of us, we hurt others when we have been hurt. People with extreme amounts of hurt, suffering and pain set out to rob others of their opportunities. This is why Americans must work together to ensure that every single American receives an equal opportunity to live a life that allows rather than prohibits individual human excellence.

Like most human beings, people who commit violent crimes against society and others were born with love and compassion in their hearts, thus destructive individuals do not always directly hurt those that are the prime sources/causes of their pain. Driven, by emotional pain, many destructive individuals take out their frustration on strangers, often without remorse. Destructive individuals probably rationalize that if they mean nothing to the people they love most, to them a stranger is of no value at all. Destructive acts, are probably, in many cases symbols of the hurt and pain that people have suffered at the hands of those intended to supply love, guidance, protection and direction. We, all of us, create the people we label monsters, the ones who commit violent crimes of pain, frustration, anger and revenge. Thus Americans must recreate a society that promotes love, respect, freedom, excellence, equality, prosperity, hard work, peace and happiness for all.

Society must share in the blame, rehabilitation and healing for the tragedies that occur in America. It is noted time and again that the people that usually wind up committing some of our most horrible crimes seem to reach the ages of twenty and thirty before committing horrible crimes. Some go through life up until their breaking points as functional, responsible adults, This should tell us that we must work to improve the processes by which we love, educate and guide ourselves and each other. It is not a rarity to hear it spoken of a person that has committed a tragic crime, that this person was nice, hardworking and likeable. For some associates, it is almost a complete surprise that the person they knew as a close friend, spouse, neighbor, co-worker or associate was capable of committing a crime-related tragedy. Somewhere along the line this person's educational system failed.

But then there are the young, troubled teenagers that don't quite reach the level in their adult lives that would allow classification as socially functional and responsible. I was able to read about some of American society's disadvantaged children in a book written by a staffer of the Covenant House, a facility that helps 28,000 homeless and runaway children every year. They provide food, clothing, shelter, medical attention, counseling, educational and vocational training. The Covenant provides help for children with no place else to go. From what I read, race, creed, color and sex was irreverent.

The book featured stories of children that had found their way to the Covenant House as a last resort for help...for survival. The book also offered various writings on assistance in dealing with young people in their teen years. This book also spoke of the teenagers that become the homeless children and teenagers of our cities. I found the following information startling, pathetic and sad.

Every 8 seconds of every school day, a child drops out of school. Every 26 seconds a child runs away from home. Every 47 seconds a child is seriously abused or neglected. Every 67 seconds a teenager has a baby. Every 7 minutes a child is arrested for drug abuse. Every 36 minutes a child is killed or injured by a gun. Every day, 135,000 American children carry their guns with them to school. Fifty-five percent of teenagers living in single-parent households live at the poverty level.

The number of teen suicides have doubled since 1970. The school dropout rate is as high as 60% in many major U.S. cities. The number of 15-year old girls who are sexually active has doubled since 1990. Ten percent of girls, ages 15 to 19, get pregnant every year. Sixty percent of all high school seniors say they have drank alcohol in the past thirty days. A District of Columbia police report found that in 1986 twenty-one percent (21%) of the people arrested on homicide charges were under twenty (20) years old. In 1990, forty-eight percent (48%) were under 20.

These statistics are tragic, sad and frightening. Adults, teenagers and children alike regardless of race, age, creed or sex must do everything we can to improve upon the generations of people we produce year after year for the successful survival of man and womankind.

Whether young or old, we all must do whatever possible to stop the on going growth of national and human tragedies suffered by old, young, rich, poor, black, and white and other nationalities. If you or someone you know is headed in a destructive or unhealthy direction, admit it and talk to someone you know about ANY problems that you may be having. Realize that you are not alone or the first to suffer emotional pain or frustration. Realize that there is a possible and workable solution to your problem. Realize as well, that no problem is too embarrassing or painful to sacrifice the necessary healing process that can spur you on to excellence and the satisfying life that we all deserve.

In 1998 Americans, should be able to reflect and say, I assisted in decreasing the negative statistics that plagued the U.S. in the early nineties. Americans must start today and maintain an on-going process for a better way of life today and for years to come for all regardless of race, sex or age. Americans must strive to establish the trials and tribulation of the nineties (and past) as memories of circumstances that no longer exist. From 1993 and beyond, Americans should strive to eliminate unemployment, poverty, violent crime, violence, racism, ignorance, discrimination, illiteracy, racial disharmony and all the other ills that make life miserable for some and unbearable for others.

Americans must establish *new* educational processes in the areas of communication, values, pride, discipline, love, acceptable behavior, compassion, and understanding almost within one year of birth that continues throughout our entire lifetimes, otherwise we will continue to raise generation after generation of individuals who grow up to become and cause the tragedies of our societies.

In 1992, an associate of mine who is a teacher of third grade children told me about a particular period of class that they have called "sharing." ("emotional sharing" should be a normal part of all of our lives) At this time, children are able to share with the class anything that may have on their minds, good or bad. The teacher told me of one child raising his hand, stating that he had something to share. He asked the question, "I wonder if I will ever see my Mother again." She asked the child, if he wanted to share with the class what had happened to his Mother.

The third grader, (eight years old) went on to say how he would watch his Mother use drugs in the basement of the home. She left one day without returning. Children of the nineties are subjected to environments that promote violence, unlawful activity and all-around misconduct. As children once teased each other about minor mishaps such as falling down or visible mucus in the nose, children now tease one another about their parents or siblings that sell drugs to one another. THIS MUST STOP! We ourselves are robbing ourselves of the life, love, liberty, freedom, happiness, peace and prosperity that we all deserve.

While children are young, we must effectively communicate with them; we must encourage and allow them to communicate with older people. We must impress the importance of respect for our elders; however we must allow young people to establish their own self-respect by the respect that we show them as young people. It is all of our jobs to raise children that grow up to be responsible and socially functional adults. As technology is increased our children are becoming aware of their environments a lot sooner that we think.

For instance, a close friend of mine has a three year old son who is enrolled in school. The child is black. He attends a school that is predominantly white. He is the only little black child in his classroom. One day, he states that he wants to have hair like one of his classmates. The father, is now forced to explain to a three year old, racial differences. The father realizes that it is extremely important that he explain to his son that though he is different, he is special and should be proud of who he is and who he will grow up to be...beautiful and black, worthy of all that life has to offer. Thus, it is never to early to start communicating with the children of the world the importance of self esteem, pride in themselves and the love that everyone should feel for them; as they are the future or our nation, our world.

Starting in 1993, among ourselves in our close knit groups, we must talk to one another as we have never communicated before. We must share our interests, our dreams, our hopes, our frustrations, our pains and concerns with one another in an effort to face our truths regardless of how ugly or beautiful they may be.

When we learn to share the misfortunes, disappointments, frustrations and pains of our personal lives, then and only then can we be able to effectively deal with our pains so as not to let them fester within, only to explode in the many faces of society and innocent victims. Likewise, we must allow ourselves to dream again, to hope again, to wish again for the best that life has to offer. It must become fashionable to establish and present to mankind the excellence in ourselves that we have buried deep inside, as a result of foolish pride.

The process of improvement must start with you and me. On all levels of society regardless of race, creed, color, age or sex we must all work together in recreating a better place for all. Honesty should be key. But, of course in a society where growth, has become phenomenal honesty becomes more and more difficult as some people find it necessary to create edges for themselves that mislead and deceive. We must admit to our ignorance and lack of education in an effort to get past that ignorance.

Taking my own advice (to admit to one's own ignorance) as the 1992 presidential election day approached, I made the conscious and responsible decision to vote. However, upon entering the voting booth, I realized, "I did not know *how* to vote." I did not understand the "punch card" procedure. I started to fake it. My tension grew. My entire body broke into a cold sweat. To myself I said, no, I will face my ignorance straight on face forward. In front of no less than ten highly professional people, I went over to the voting assistant and told her, I don't know *how* to vote. She tried to explain the procedure to me. Courageously, I said, I still don't understand, will go in there with me. She complied. I felt proud that I had voted in the 1992 presidential election. But I felt more proud of the fact that I had faced my ignorance straight on and face forward. All the "saved" embarrassment in the world is not worth holding on to ignorance.

Since I am on the topic of "governmental process", I would like to say as an average American, black woman, I am a little disappointed in Jessie Jackson. (a persuasive black man on a national level since 1966) I found it a little disappointing, however, that after the announcement of Magic Johnson's retirement from basketball as a result of the HIV Virus, Jessie Jackson within days appeared on the front page of the local Detroit Newspaper with his intent to hold an Aid's Summit. I felt it was a direct ploy for some of the attention that Magic had garnered. So did a lot of my peers as I wanted to know what impression they had of Jessie Jackson. Most felt that he had become an opportunist. After several months, I heard no mention of Jessie Jackson's name in any way regarding Aids. Why?

Jessie Jackson has, no doubt done great deeds in the struggles for all people, however, with all his notoriety and supposed purpose, I feel

253

he could be doing more. Why has Jessie Jackson not written a book so that people can have in their possessions "his message" or philosophy. Jessie Jackson has been one of the more prominent black male figures of America. It should be historically documented what his message and philosophy is to the American people about life in America. "Tell us Mr. Jackson, what is it *REALLY* like for a black man to run for the Presidency of the United States of America?" "What three things should a young black male/female know or do if he ever wanted to become the President of the United States?" Will a black man/woman ever be elected as President of the United States of America? Is a black person qualified to run the United States of America? Who? When? Why?

In the nineties, as America and the rest of the world is in a deep state of debt, confusion, corruption and depression, a great many other ills, it is now necessary for ALL of us (regardless of race, sex or age) to *seriously* ask and demand more of ourselves and each other in improving the state of things now and in the years to come. As the new President, Bill Clinton (1992) offers a mandate for change, all Americans must assist the president in bringing about positive changes. Regardless of how successful a president is in providing opportunities for change, circumstances in America will remain bleak, if Americans sit back and wait for opportunities and rewards to be dropped in their laps. Just as any president, *hopefully*, works for the betterment of life in America, Americans themselves must work equally as hard to contribute to their own well-being, prosperity and upward mobility.

In my opinion, far too many black males are socially, intellectually and economically passive. As a young black woman of the nineties, I sincerely feel that it is in large part the black woman's fault for the lazy, passive and economically deficient attitude of many black males...thus it is the black woman who must also accept the consequences of the depressive and oppressive plight of blacks. But moreover it is the black woman who must change how she interacts with the black male. Black females/women must conduct and carry themselves in ways that influence, assist and insist that black males strive to reach their full manhood potential. Black males of the nineties, by the masses, will never become men if they continue to operate in the same irresponsible, undisciplined, uncommitted way in which many live their lives in the nineties.

Almost every time a tally is taken, black men come in dead last, particularly in the areas of finance and or upward mobility. No real man should be comfortable with this. Black men fail to realize that in their heavy concentration on recreational activity and non-productive activity they are continuously chipping away at their manhood, as individuals and as a race of *potential* men. Steadfastedly holding on to their reputations in the area of sexuality, black males stand very tall, but they fall very short in the areas that matter most. Black males are failing the black race and thus the human race as role models, fathers, teachers, leaders, employers, employees, hence all of America suffers.

When women allow black males to be lazy, irresponsible and careless they aid them in disrespecting themselves as *potential* men. Unfortunately, a lot of males are not aware of the damage they cause themselves as they shirk responsibility, run from commitment and maintain rampant ignorance in the areas of politics, financial security, personal growth and overall social consciousness. Black men, as well as men of other races have gotten so far removed from the responsibilities, morals, values and ethics of manhood some no longer even no what manhood means, thus millions of adult males do not have the slightest idea of what is expected of them as men.

And naturally younger males that follow in the footsteps of males who never become men, create and perpetuate the tragedies of males who become absent fathers, unemployable, drug addicts, habitual criminals and negative statistics in America. Realizing and suffering the consequences of men with boyish minds, attitudes and behavior patterns, all women must assist men in establishing, defining and developing constructive behavior patterns that contribute to their development as men.

As a black woman, I say all that I have said not to bash black men. I realize that if circumstances are to improve we have to start with the truth. We all have to lay our strengths AND weaknesses on the table to be dealt with before we can reach the necessary solutions to heal the wounds that have needlessly destroyed far too many lives. I think we all agree, that as we proceed into the nineties, we all have a lot of weaknesses and all of America is in great need of improvement. As a black woman I can constructively focus on the weaknesses of the black race because I am black. People of other races must deal with their racial deficiencies as they are more apt to understand the problems and what is necessary to make positive changes.

Blacks compose only 12 percent of the population. Yet, blacks make up 62 percent of those who are poor and remain poor. This statistic should be unacceptable to all blacks and all blacks should be working together to eliminate poverty within the black race, as well as in America. We get these results because there has been a growing tendency for black males to drop out of the work force entirely." The illiteracy rate for blacks is 22 percent; a figure that should drop to zero (0) by the year 2000. It is projected that the percentage of black males in the workforce (ages 16-24) will fall from 62 percent in 1986 to 53 percent in 1995. It is projected that 77 percent of white males will be in the workforce in 1995. Blacks and males should prove these statistics to be WRONG? All able-bodied males of working age, unless they are in school should be employed, with a company or working in a company that he has created and is growing to a level to provide for a satisfactory living standard for himself and others.

Almost 3.7 million new businesses were started in the U.S. between 1981-1986. Per 1,000 persons, 63 percent of the new business were started by whites. Only 12 percent of the new businesses were started by blacks.

Blacks/African Americans should be ashamed of these differences. As a black person myself, blacks cannot continue to complain of unemployment opportunities, if blacks continue to be unconcerned about CREATING job opportunities for themselves AND others. Yes, it is realized that racism, bigotry and discrimination are still alive and well in America in the nineties. However, blacks are intelligent and shrewd enough to work around these obstacles, as they simultaneously work to

257

eliminate racism in America and around the world. If blacks worked to establish viable businesses that are vital to the strength of America, racism, bigotry and discrimination would eliminate itself as white America, in particular, would quickly realize the need and advantages of workable relationships with blacks and their businesses.

When I talk to young blacks males about the possibilities of creating or contributing to society beyond their nine to fives, they no longer want to talk. But then they are quick to whine, cry and wonder why they always get the short end of the stick. Blacks will remain, oppressed, depressed, isolated, alienated as long as they continue waiting for opportunities, rather than creating opportunities and pretending to have it all together while living hand to mouth and from paycheck to paycheck.

Black males friends call and ask, "what are you doing?" I reply, "I'm working. They say, "Oh, that's too bad." I say, "no, your attitude is what's bad." "They say, "what do you mean." I say, "never mind, you'll learn." Black men, should collectively challenge themselves to reverse the negative reputations that they have created for themselves. In the next year or two or even five years anyone should be able to pick up this book, compare it with new data and see remarkable *positive* changes in how blacks fare in the broad scheme of the American portrait. Significantly, black men should stop playing with black women and start working with them.

A certain gentleman, came to a major Corporation to introduce a book that he had written. No doubt, he also agrees and sees that there is a need for change and improvement.

258

The title of the book was The United States of
Incompetency or something to that effect. I
wanted to address one particular statement that
he made during a one hour reading from his
book. To be precise and accurate, I thought it
would be best if I bought a copy. BUT after
trying several book stores, I was disappointed
to find it was not available. If this man was
serious, sincere and thoroughly competent
regarding his message, he should have made
sure that copies were available before coming
to a major corporation. With me one sale was
lost...and no doubt many others.

In agreement with the author's message of
demanding excellence and improved
competency, I also feel it is important that we
realize that we are all human, we all make
mistakes, misjudgments, miscalculations and
oversights. None of us is perfect. However, we
must all strive to always do our best toward
achieving personal, national and universal
excellence.

The statement, that I wish to address was that
"*one should not falter in demanding
competency for fear of being called a racist.*" I
interpreted his demand for competency as a
call to improve upon the state of things in
America. I too agree that America is steadily
losing her grip on things once taken for
granted like prosperity, employment, peaceful
and quality living. To me, for this author to
make such a statement, (regarding racism), I
feel compelled to present the other side of the
coin. Especially, if he is serious about actually
bringing about a total, overall improvement
for ALL of America; which must happen if
America is to restore "The Great American
Dream." There is side of the coin that he and
many others may not be aware of or may not
wish to deal with or address.

The other side of the coin: From a black working woman's perspective, a lot of black talent, capabilities, intelligence, and ability is stifled, pushed under the table, shoved into drawers and sometimes completely destroyed by racial intimidation and monopolizing. I will not go into great detail, but tremendous barriers exist for racially motivated reasons. To call it just as it is, whites are cordial, friendly and most often team players. But for some *odd* reason, they often show undeniable signs of discomfort when blacks demonstrate progress, growth and high intellectual potential within the workforces whereby blacks are the minority. Often when these circumstances occur, very quiet, subtle and refined roadblocks are erected to stop, stifle, ignore or even destroy the possibility of black excellence in the workplace. Yes, it is quite evident that blacks have made great strides and made major contributions to the strength of modern America, however, much has been done to limit black excellence in America.

When serious issues are tabled are discussed, whites often come across as though they truly believe that blacks are stupid and are not the adults that whites are, thereby justifying mutual respect, compromise and effective communication.

If circumstances in America are to improve for all the intelligence, capabilities and abilities of blacks must cease to be stifled and denied. This type of action and behavior is usually executed and maintained by whites in authority that wish to continue to believe that all blacks are inferior, ignorant and cannot possibly be right about anything they say or do. It also seems that the talents of blacks *are* recognized but black excellence is stifled out of racially motivated envy and insecurity on the part of whites. Just as whites attempt to convince blacks that racism and bigotry does not exist and if it surfaces, whites are quick to ask, "could it be that the racism that you *think* you feel, is just you imagination?" I cannot truly understand how nor why persons with racist attitudes believe and think as they do. One day I would like to publicly, openly, calmly and rationally discuss with a professional white person who claims to hate all blacks. (simply because they are black) I would like to understand their reasons and motivations behind their feelings of racial hatred toward blacks.

To me whites should ashamed of their racist attitudes as I feel that racism is the subconscious fear of one's own feelings of inferiority and insecurity. If we want to see things improve for the entire human race and all our nations, we must all destroy our own inferiority complexes. The root of all jealousy, racism, sexism and bigotry evolves out of our deep rooted (gut) feelings of insecurity and low-level self-esteem.

Most everyone has or will come face to face with someone who is perceived to be prettier, more handsome, smarter, richer, taller, shorter, thinner or simply more self-confident. It cannot be denied that almost all of us at some point in our lives will feel inferior, if even for a moment. Be honest with yourself. Individuals with well-balanced attitudes about themselves can accept the fact that there is someone with whom they might like to trade attributes, assets, physical characteristics or entire places; but realizing that they can not, healthy, well-balanced and intelligent individuals proceed with their lives striving for their own personal excellence, which may, one day even surpass the object of past jealous or inferiority complex provoking feelings. While on the other hand, people with unhealthy attitudes about themselves tend to dwell and focus on the positive characteristics of others, wishing to be what they are not rather than striving to reach a personal conscious level whereby they can feel happy, satisfied and proud of who or what they are.

We must admit to and eliminate personal insecurities so that we all can openly welcome, accept and appreciate the talents, capabilities, intelligence and accomplishment of all people regardless of race, creed, age, sex or color. America and the rest of the world would be a much better place for all if we all, from this day forward, commit to the total destruction of personal insecurity and inferiority--as we strive for individual, national and universal excellence.

It is not a rarity for some blacks to put forth extreme energies to prove their talents, intelligence and capabilities--while others put forth the same energies to squelch black efforts. However, it must be realized that as we intentionally block others from their pursuits of happiness and prosperity, we in turn create the monsters who rob and kill, overwhelmed by frustration and angers as a result of being suppressed, oppressed, separated and alienated.

It cannot be denied that America was built as a result of hard work, a whole lot of pain and a great many contributions by black men and black woman. Blacks allow themselves to feel inferior and frustrated because they themselves do not fully acknowledge, realize and actively communicate the contributions that they, as a people, have made to America.

CHAPTER FOUR

HISTORICALLY GREAT BLACK WOMEN

This chapter chronicles just a few of the contributions that black women (the so called weaker sex) have made to America; making it what it is...the greatest and most powerful country in the world. In that America is weakening in a great many areas, one must go back to the black woman for assistance in the rebuilding of America's strength, hopes and dreams.

This chapter illustrates the strength and fortitude of black American women who suffered great pains in paving the roads that we in the nineties travel and take for granted. In the nineties, we, with all our privileges, freedoms, knowledge and experience tire sometimes at the mention of work or the thought of going an extra mile. If it had not been for the contributions of these black women, we could not enjoy many of the luxuries that we all enjoy today.

1917-1977 Fannie Lou Hamer--Founder and Vice-Chairwoman of the Mississippi Freedom Democratic Party. This woman was the last of twenty (20) children. (We complain of our family's of five) Her parents were sharecroppers. In her attempts to vote in 1962, she was badly beaten, shot at abused, jailed and threatened to be killed. Dr. Martin Luther King demanded her release from Jail. In 1964, two years later, obviously without destructive grudge, Fannie Lou was the first black woman to run for Congress from the Second District of Mississippi. She raised over one million dollars for Sunflower County. Still untiring,

Fannie Lou established a 680 acre complex called the Freedom Farmer Cooperative. This complex housed and fed the poor of all races. Moreover she founded a Day Care Center for the children of working mothers.

1842-1924 Josephine St. Pierre Ruffin--Civic Leader and Black Women's Club Organizer. Instrumental in publishing the first Black Women's Newspaper in the United States.

1866-1923--Mary Burnett Talbert--Educator, Red Cross Nurse during WWI and Civil Rights Advocate. Received Bachelor's degree at nineteen in 1886. Helped fight the war on racial prejudices and discrimination.

960-930 B.C. Makeda (Ma-Kee'-Da)--African Queen. The legendary Queen of Sheba. This woman was Queen of both Ethiopia and Saba in Southern Arabia. Axum the capital city of her empire was believed to be founded 100 years after the flood. Makeda was very rich and very beautiful. The Queen of Sheba traveled to Jerusalem to learn from King Soloman, a very wise man. The queen of Sheba gave birth to a son fathered by King Soloman of Israel.

1803-1879 Marie W. Steward--Generally acknowledged as the first American born woman to lecture in public. She spoke on issues concerning Black economic advancement, the abolition of slavery and African pride. Her first speech was made in Boston in 1832. Her parents died when she was only five years old. She challenged "daughters of Africa" to use resources to uplift the Black race.

1938--Crystal Bird Fauslet--Elected to the Pennsylvania State Assembly in 1938. She was

the first black woman elected to a <u>mayor's</u>
<u>public office in the United States.</u>

<u>1895-1911 Mary Church Terrell</u>--was the first
black woman to serve on a school board.   From
(1895-1991) she served two terms on the
<u>Washington D.C. School Board.</u>

<u>Mary McCleod Bethune</u>--served as advisor and
Confidante to President Franklin Roosevelt.
She was regularly called upon to confer and
advise the President.   President Franklin
Roosevelt was so impressed with her
capabilities that he created the <u>Office of</u>
<u>Minority Affairs of the National Youth</u>
<u>Administration</u>--Mary McCleod Bethune was
named administrator.

<u>Ethelene Crockett</u>--the first black woman
<u>Obstetrician-Gynecologist</u> in Michigan.
Ethelene was the first woman National
President of the American Lung Association.
Ethelene Crockett was the wife of Judge George
Crockett.

<u>Ida Mae J. Hiram 1890</u>--The first black woman
to pass the Georgia State Dental Board.   Ida Mae
Hiram was the only woman <u>dentist</u> in the State
of Georgia in 1910.

<u>Mary Jane Watkins</u>--the first <u>woman</u> dentist in
the military services.   Mary Jane Watkins
received her Doctor of Dental Surgery degree
in 1924.

<u>1913--Daisy Hill Northcross</u>--received a
medical degree from Lajola Medical Collegen in
Chicago, Illinois.   Daisy Hill Northcross was the
Founder of <u>Detroit Mercy Hospital of Detroit,</u>
<u>Michigan</u>.

265

<u>1923--Effie O. Ellis</u>--was the first black person to hold an administrative position with the <u>American Medical Association.</u> Effie O. Ellis was named special assistant to the Executive Vice-President. She graduated from Spelman College and the University of Illinois Medical School.

<u>Dorothy McClendon</u>--<u>Micro-biologist</u> for twenty-four years. Coordinator of microbiological research for the U.S. Army Tank Command (TACOM) Developer of methods to prevent micro-organisms from contaminating fuel and deteriorating fuel and deteriorating military storage material. As a Detroit teenager she attended <u>Cass Technical High School</u>. Dorothy McClendon received awards for scientific Achievement from the Michigan Society of Professional Engineers, The Detroit Central Business District Association and Tennessee Agricultural and Industrial State University.

<u>1867--Madame C. J. Walker</u>--Made a fortune from her invention of the straightening comb. She was born December 23, 1867. This woman was definitely not born with a silver spoon, in her mouth or anyplace else in sight. Madame C. J. Walker lost both her parents when she was six years old. By the age of fourteen she was married. By the age of twenty, she was a widow with a child to support. By 1915, she the largest business owner of New York. Madame C. J. Walker employed more than five-hundred people across the U.S. She was the first Black Woman in modern times to build a manufacturing enterprise. She also founded laboratories in Indianapolis to develop her beauty products. The company that Madame C. J. Walker founded, eventually employed more than three thousand people. This pioneering

Black Woman opened up career opportunities for Black Women who may not have gotten such opportunities had it not be for Madame C. J. Walker Madame C. J. Walker died as the Black Woman millionaire of 1919.

1903--Maggie L. Walker--the first female bank owner. Maggie L. Walker formed the St. Luke's Penny Savings Bank. The name was changed to the Saint Luke's Bank and Trust Company in 1903. She was the first woman bank president in America. Maggie L. Walker was the daughter of a house slave born in 1867. Additionally, this great Black Woman established a Black Newspaper. The Newspaper was called the St. Luke Herald. She also founded a school for Black Girls.

Carole Hoover--The First Bank National Association of Cleveland, Ohio was established. Carole Hoover acted as Deputy Organizer. This Bank ranked sixth among Black Banks. Assets totaled more than $34 million. In 1976, 167,000 loans were processed totaling $8 million.

Mary Ellen Pleasant--1800's--The Black woman was credited as the best business person (male or female) in San Francisco. Mary Ellen Pleasant described herself as a "capitalist by profession." As a housekeeper, Mary Ellen Pleasant speculated in the stock and money markets. It was speculated that she was born in slavery. By 1855 she owned a string of laundries. In 1867 or 1868, Mary Ellen opened her first boarding house. 'pyramiding" her profits, she became the managing director of several boarding houses and restaurants. In 1890 and 1891, Mary Ellen Pleasant bought and created a 1,000 acre ranch in Sonoma County, California. Mary Ellen Pleasant died in 1904.

<u>Mary McCleod Bethune</u>--Well known educator. Mary McCleod Bethune was also a land developer. She was also the director of substantial Florida businesses.

<u>Carol A. Bond</u>--1974--With $600, the Black Woman founded C. A. Bonds and Associates. This company was founded as a management and consulting firm in Springfield, Illinois. After one year alone, Carol A. Bond secured more than seventy thousand dollars in contracts. During that same year (1974) Carol A. Bond quit her job as a computer programmer with the Illinois Department of Registration and Education. In just one year, this phenomenal Black Woman quadrupled her annual income.

<u>Bessie May Weaver</u>--1911--In this year, (1911) this Black Woman became the only Black florist in Kansas, City Missouri. She founded and managed the Weaver Floral Company.

<u>Gwendolyn Hooker</u>--1938--Of Portland Oregon, Gwendolyn Hooker established the first Black Woman owned flower shop. She continued to operate the shop through the age of 78.

<u>Cora Walker</u>--1968--The courageous Black Woman organized a cooperative supermarket in Harlem. The cooperative supermarket was community owned and supported by more than 4,000 shareholders. This cooperative supermarket allowed the supported to share in the profits. The effort was an expanding business enterprise. The cooperative supermarket provided the chance to learn the fundamentals (duties/responsibilities/functions) of supermarket operation--on the job training.

<u>Wanda Babin</u> --1972--Los Angeles California.
This Black Woman founded and presided over
the Eagle Guardian Security and Patrol Service.
Gross sales for the first year of business was
$75,000. In 1977 Wanda Babin's company
grossed $500,000. She employed a staff of 25
security guards.

<u>Charlotte Ray</u>--1872--This pioneering great
Black Woman was the first Black Woman to
graduate from a law school. Charlotte Ray
graduated from Howard Law School in 1872.

<u>Matilda Bolin</u>--1908--The first Black American
woman judge in the United States.

<u>Margorie M. Lawson</u>--This Black Woman was
noted for being the first Black woman
appointed to a judgeship by a president of the
United States. That president was John F.
Kennedy. The appointment occurred in 1962.

<u>Selma Burke</u>--1901--Pioneering Black Female
Artist. No doubt you are in possession of a
work of art by this famous Black Woman. The
portrait of President Roosevelt that appears on
a Roosevelt dime, was taken from a plaque
sculpted buy, none other than Selma Burke. In
1944 the Fine Arts Committee for Washington,
D.C invited sculptors to compete for the honor
of making a plaque of President Roosevelt to be
placed in a government Building. Ms. Selma
Burke, a Black Woman, won the honor.
Congratulations. Her art work lives on and on.

<u>Constance Baker Motley</u>--1912--Attended
college at Fisk University and New York
University. In 1963 Mrs. Motley ran for a set
in the New York State Senate. She won. Mrs.
Constance Baker Motley became the only
woman in the Senate. President John

appointed Mrs. Motley as federal judge for the Southern District of New York. She was the first woman to be appointed a federal judge.

Oprah Winfrey 1990's--Multi-Multi--millionairess. Talk Show Host. TV-Movie Star. One of America's most successful and renown Black Women. At the age of 15, she wanted to always be the best person she could be. She works very hard. She is one of the best of the best. A role model and a hero. I have had many instances to hear black men refer to Oprah in unflattering terms. To me this is a sign that these men are only jealous of her success, fortitude, fame and all the other wonderful attributes attributed to Oprah Winfrey. It is wildly beyond me how any Black person that makes less than $30,000 could say anything subjectively negative about this already great, pioneering woman. She should be an inspiration and beacon of hope for all people of African or Black American Descent. Oprah Winfrey is a symbol of what we all are capable of--successful living. We should all be proud of her.

Vanessa Williams--Former Miss American Queen--This beautiful black woman rose to the top of America through talent, physical and inner beauty. She was the first Black Woman to be crowned "Miss America". Though fate would have her stumble she rose again to regain another crown as singer, video and film star. She is a perfect example that against all odds "victory" can be yours.

Janet Jackson 1990's--Another Black Multi-Multi-Millionairesss--with a message. With her creation of "Rhythm Nation 1814" "she pleads to all people to attend to the world's painful wounds." Janet Jackson is beautiful inside and out. On her Rhythm Nation Video she states that if one wants something bad enough you have to "work for it." And that she definitely does. It is obvious in watching her strenuous song and dance routines that this is a strong Black Woman, determined and driven to fight--for perfection, to win. "Bravo Janet!"

<u>Carol Mosley Braun</u>-1992-First Black Woman nominated for the U.S. Senate by a major Party. Defeated two well-financed white male opponents. Fourth Black American to serve in the Senate.

<u>Mae C. Jemison</u>-1992-A physician, first Black Woman in outer space.

<u>Leah J. Sears-Collins</u>-1992-Elected to the Georgia Supreme Court. She is the first woman, second Black American and youngest justice in the history of the state's high court. Age-37.

<u>Terry McMillan</u>-1992-Best Selling Author for "Waiting To Exhale." Paperback rights sold for $2.64 million, one of the largest sums ever paid for reprint rights.

<u>Robin Givens</u>, <u>Lynn Whitfield</u>, <u>Sheryl Lee Ralph</u>, <u>Kimberly Russell</u>, <u>Vanessa Calloway</u>, <u>Janet Hubert-Whitten</u>--Film and Television Actresses (1990's)--I applaud you all for breaking into this difficult industry. But as strong, talented experienced, intelligent, wealthy, black women, there is absolutely NO reason for you to complain that 'HOLLYWOOD' is not *giving* enough work to black actresses. This observation is a result of an article that appeared in the June 1991, issue of Ebony Magazine. It is further a cop out to except that the white males that run Hollywood lack

271

imagination and vision where black women are concerned.

The black female actresses and entertainers of this country, together have enough experience, money AND talent to write, produce, direct, market, act and control your own projects. You already have a start and the attention of America. Look at what Spike Lee has done. Create your own employment vehicles and quit waiting for Hollywood hand-outs.
If you need some help--I would be more than happy to lend a hand in writing, acting and or directing. Based on my own life experiences, I have quite a few story lines that might interest you. If I, with absolutely no experience in the film and TV industry, can feel this way, certainly all of you can turn your wants, needs and desires into "lights, cameras and most importantly "ACTION". Form a group, a company, work together, pool your resources and tap into them. If you cannot adequately break into the already established "industry" start your own. Talk to some of the black women featured in the article "Black Women at the Top In TV". This article is featured in the Ebony, June 1991, edition. As I have said before, we all (especially blacks) must quit relying on a select few to satisfy the needs of millions. It is an impossible task. NOW, beautiful black actresses, let's see what you can come up with. Challenge yourselves. stretch. Reach! Ask Whoopi Goldberg to help you...from the outside looking in, she is brilliant...so are the black female actresses of "A Different World." (Bill Cosby)

In my life, as a black woman, living and born in America, these are just a few of the role models, heroes and inspirations that I have adopted either through the written word, television or live entertainment. I have only met one of the black women that I have chronolized, yet all these black women are examples of what all black women are meant to be--successful and great.

The chapter that follows provide a small sampling of job opportunities and professions available in the United States of America. They are provided to assistant anyone in locating the pathway to his or her own purpose in life.

CHAPTER FIVE
OPTIONS AND OPPORTUNITIES

This chapter is written to provide guidance, in choosing or locating a career path that is closest in line with your strengths and weaknesses, your likes and dislikes, your goals and aspirations. This chapter also takes into consideration social factors that influence the job market.

Though I may provide information that is readily available and easy to obtain, we all realize that sometimes the messenger of a common message can make all the difference in the world.

Provided by the Bureau of Labor Statistic, U.S. Department of Labor, obtained from the book "America's New Economy--The Basic Guide" is a table that provides the projected changes in employment between the year of 1986-2000.

Most New Jobs	New Jobs	% Change
Retail Sales	1,200,000	33%
Waiter/Waitress	752,000	44%
Nursing	612,000	44%
Janitor	604,000	23%
General Manager	582,000	24%
Cashier	575,000	26%
Truck Driver	525,000	24%
Office Clerk	462,000	20%
Food Counter Worker	449,000	30%
Nursing Aide	443,000	35%

Fastest Growing	New Jobs	% Change
Para-legal	64,000	104%
Medical Assistant	119,000	90%
Physical Therapist	53,000	87%

Computer Repair	56,000	81%
Home Health Aide	111,000	80%
Systems Analyst	251,000	76%

Most Rapidly Declining	Lost Jobs	% Change
Electrical Assemblers	-116,000	-54%
Electronic Processors	-14,000	-51%
Railroad Conductors	-17,000	-41%
Shoe Assemblers	-18,000	-32%
Telephone Installers	-40,000	-32%
Chemical Equip. Tech.	-52,000	-30%
Chemical Plant Oper.	-23,000	-30%

What follows is a small example of career paths and opportunities available. This information was taken from the Occupational Outlook Handbook by the U.S. Department of Labor Bureau of Labor statistics.

I think it is crucial that any person seeking to determine a career path should research for themselves the responsibilities, duties, the advancement opportunities and pay scales relative to any profession that may be considered.

It is the responsibility of the individual to determine what type of person you are. One should then choose a profession that would best enhance, develop all personal qualities and talents. Also of primary importance is the determination of the type of life style one wishes to live. Will the career path you choose satisfy your lifelong hopes, dreams and desires? Successful living can be yours if you take control and responsibility for your own happiness and success. Couple your actions with undying commitment, determination, strength, fortitude, belief in yourself and a winning attitude and you will successful.

Executive, Administrative and Managerial Occupations

Accountants and Auditors--Accountants and auditors prepare, analyze and verify financial reports in ALL business, industrial and government organizations. Accountants and auditors also work for local governments. Accountants and auditors summarize transactions in standard formats for financial records. The data is put in special formats that aid in financial or managerial analysis. Accountants and auditors also prepare income tax returns. Accountants and auditors work in offices. Self employed accountants may be able to work out of their homes. Accountants and auditors employed by large firms and government agencies may travel to perform audits at clients' places of business, branch offices or government facilities. Accountants and auditors held about 963,000 jobs in 1988. Most public accounting and business firms require applicants for accountant and internal auditor positions to have at least a bachelor's degree in accounting or a closely related field.

Employment of accountants and auditors is expected to grow faster than the average for all occupations through the year 2000 due to the key role that accountants and auditors play in the management of all types of businesses. According to a 1989 College Placement Council Salary Survey, bachelor degree candidates in accounting received starting salary offers averaging $25,300. Salaries of junior public accountants who were not owners or partners of the firms averaged $26,600. Some had salaries of more than $38,000. Owners and partners of firms earned more. Accountants and auditors employed by the Federal

Government averaged about $36,400 a year in 1988.

Education Administrators--Education administrators provide direction leadership and day to day management of educational activities in schools, colleges, universities, businesses, correctional institutions, museums, and job training and community service organization. Education administrators set educational standards and goals. They set up policies and procedures to carry them out. Education administrators held about 320,000 jobs in 1988. Education administration is not usually an entry level job. Most begin their careers in other related occupations. Employment of education administration is expected to grow as fast as the average for all occupations through the year 2000. The median annual salary for education administrators who worked full time in 1988 was $35,000. The middle fifty percent earned between $23,000 and $45,000.

Government Chief Executives and Legislators-- The government tells U.S. citizens what to do. Chief executives and legislators at the Federal, State and local level tells the government what to do. Chief executives are officials in charge of units of government who carry out and enforce laws. They include the President, and Vice President of the United States, State governors and lieutenant governors, county commissioners, township supervisors, mayors and city managers. All except city and county managers are elected. Managers are appointed by the city council and the county commission.

Legislators are the elected officials who make laws or amend existing one in order to remedy problems or to promote certain activities.

They include U.S. Senators, and Representatives, State Senators and Representatives (called assemblymen or delegates in some States) and county legislatures and city and town council members (called aldermen or selectmen in some areas). Both chief executives and legislators perform ceremonial duties--they open new structures and businesses; make proclamations, welcome visitors and lead celebrations. Chief executives and legislators held about 69,000 jobs in 1988. About four of five worked in local government. The rest worked in the Federal and State governments. The Federal Government had 535 Senators and Representatives. State legislators totaled approximately 7,500. City managers approximately 4,900. Most chief executives and legislators are elected. Voters determine whether an individual who meets the minimum age and citizenship requirements of the position is fit to hold it. "The question is not how does one become qualified?' The question is "How does one get elected?" The earning of public administrators vary widely, depending on the size of the government unit and on whether the job is part time, full time, year round or full time for a few months a year.

Engineers--Engineers apply the theories and principles of science and mathematics to the economical solution of practical technical problems. Engineers design machinery, products, systems and processes for efficient and economical performance. In 1986 engineers held almost 1,411,000 jobs. Various types of engineers include: electrical, mechanical, civil, industrial, aerospace, chemical, metallurgical, petroleum, nuclear, etc. A bachelor's degree in engineering form an accredited engineering program is generally acceptable for beginning engineering jobs. Employment opportunities in engineering have been good for a numb of years. Opportunities are expected to continue to be good through the year 2000. Employment is expected to increase faster than the average for all occupations. Starting salaries for engineers with the bachelors degree are significantly higher than starting salaries of college graduates in other fields. According to the College Placement Council, engineering graduates with a bachelor's degree averaged about $29,200 a year in private industry in 1988. Experienced middle level engineers with no supervisory responsibilities averaged $45,777. The average salary for engineers in the Federal Government was about $42,300 in 1988.

Pharmacists--Pharmacists advise the public on the proper selection and use of medicine. They also dispense drugs and medicines prescribed by health practitioners such as physicians, pediatrist and dentists. Pharmacists in hospitals and clinics dispense medications and advise the medical staff on the selection and effects of drugs. Pharmacists held about 162,000 jobs in 1988. A license to practice pharmacy is required in all states. Employment of pharmacists is expected to grow faster than the average for all occupations through the year 2000 mainly due to the increased pharmaceutical needs of a larger and older population. Median annual earnings of full-time, salaried pharmacists were $37,366 in 1988. Pharmacists working in chain drug stores had an average base salary of $41,800 per year.

Radio and Television Announcers and Newscasters--Announcers and newscasters are well-known personalities to radio and

279

television audiences. Radio announcers often called disk jockeys, select and introduce recorded music, present news, sports, weather and commercials, interview guests and report on community activities and other matter of interest to their audience. Announcers at larger stations usually specialize in sports or weather or in general news and may be called newscasters or anchors. Radio and television announcers and newscasters held about 57,000 jobs in 1988. Formal training in broadcast journalism from a college or technical school is valuable. Station officials pay particular attention to taped auditions that show an applicant's delivery. Those hired by television stations usually start out as production secretaries, production assistants, researchers or reporters. Employment of announcers is expected to increase about as fast as the average for all occupations through the year 2000 as new radio and TV stations are licensed and the number of cable television systems continues to grow. Salaries in broadcasting vary widely. They are higher in television than in radio, higher in larger markets than in small ones and higher in commercial than in public broadcasting. The success of announcers and news broadcasters depends upon how well they speak to their audiences.

Reporters and Correspondents--Reporters and correspondents play a key role in our society. They gather information and prepare stories that inform us about local, state, national and international events. They present points of view on current issues; and monitor the actions of public officials, corporate executives, special interest groups and others who exercise power. Reporters in radio and television broadcasting often compose their story and report "live" from the scene of a newsworthy event. Reporters and correspondents held about 70,000 jobs in 1988. About 7 of every 10 worked for newspapers. Almost two in ten worked in radio and TV broadcasting and others worked for magazines and wire services. Employment of reports and correspondents is expected to grow about as fast as the average for all occupations through the year 2000. This growth will come about primarily because of an anticipated increase in the number of small town and suburban daily and weekly newspapers. Annual salaries of radio reports ranged from about $12,000 in the smaller stations to about $30,000 in the largest stations in 1988. According to a survey conducted by the National Association of Broadcasters, salaries of TV reporters ranged from about $15,000 in the smallest stations to about $67,400 in the largest ones.

<u>Writers and Editors</u> Writers and editors communicate through the written word. Writers develop original fiction and non fiction for books, magazines, trade journals, newspapers, technical studies and reports, company newsletters, radio and television broadcasts, record companies and advertisements. Established writers may work on a freelance basis, where they sell their work to publishers or publication units, manufacturing firms and public relations and advertising departments or agencies.

Editors frequently do some writing. They almost always rewrite and edit. Primary duties are to plan the contents of books, magazines or newspapers and to supervise their preparation. Writers and editors held about 219,000 jobs in 1988. Nearly 40 percent of salaried writers and editors work for newspapers, magazines and book publishers. Jobs with major book publishers, magazines, broadcasting companies, advertising agencies and public relations firms and the Federal Government are concentrated in new York, Chicago, Los Angeles, Boston, Philadelphia, San Francisco and Washington D.C.

Employment of writers and editors is expected to increase faster than the average for all occupations through the year 2000. Employment of salaried writers and editors by newspapers, periodicals, book publishers and nonprofit organizations is expected to increase with growing demand for their publications. Demand for technical writers is expected to increase because of the continuing expansion of scientific and technical information and the continued need to communicate it. In 1988, beginning salaries for writers and editorial assistants ranged from $18,000 to $26,600 annually according to the Sales and Marketing Personnel Report 3rd Edition, 1988/89 published by the Executive Compensation Service, a Wyatt Data Services Company. Technical writers had salaries ranging from $19,800 to $46,300. Senior editors on large circulation newspapers and magazines averaged over $50,000 per year. Writers and editors employed by the Federal Government earned an average of $31,228 a year in 1888.

Visual Arts Occupations
Designers--Designers organize and design articles, products and materials in such a way that they not only serve the purpose for which they were intended but are visually pleasing as well. Designers usually specialize in one particular area of design, for example automobiles, (what I do for my base living) clothing, furniture, home appliances,

industrial equipment, movie and theater sets, packaging or floral arrangements.

Design is a number of different fields. Industrial designers develop and design countless manufactured products like cars, home appliances, computers, stethoscopes, filing cabinets, fishing rods, pens, and piggy banks. Designers combine artistic talent with research or product use, marketing, materials and production methods to create the best and most appealing design and to make the product competitive with others in the marketplace.

Designers held about 309,000 jobs in 1988. It is highly recommended that students in the design field take computer aided design (CAD) courses--fun, quick and easy to learn. Cad is used in many design areas, particularly in industrial design. Employers expect new employees to be familiar with the use of the computer as a design tool. (I love computers) Computers are used extensively in the aerospace, automotive and electronic industries and are becoming more popular in the other design fields.

Employment in design occupations is expected to grow faster than the average for all occupations through the year 2000. Median annual earnings of experienced full-time designers were about $26,400 in 1988. The middle fifty percent earned between $16,700 and $35,00 a year. The bottom ten percent earned less than $11,300 and the top ten percent earned more than $47,000. Male dominated occupation.
Visual Artists--Visual artists use an almost limitless variety of methods and materials to communicate ideas, thoughts and feelings. They may use oils, watercolors, acrylics, pastels magic markers, pencils, pen and ink,

silk-screen, plaster, clay or any of a number of other methods to create abstract works or images of objects, people, nature topography or events. Graphic artists perform different jobs depending on their area of expertise. There are graphic designers, illustrators, editorial artists, medical and scientific illustrators, fashion artists, cartoonists and animators. Visual artists held about 216,000 jobs in 1988. About three out of five were self-employed. Visual artists are concentrated in large cities. New York City has the largest concentration because it is the center of both advertising and publishing. Boston, Chicago, Los Angeles, and San Francisco also have many artists. The graphic and fine arts fields have a glamorous and exciting image. Formal entry qualifications are few. People with a love for drawing and creative ability qualify for entry. Employment of visual artists, overall is expected to grow faster than average for all occupations through the year 2000. Demand for work of graphic artists will be strong as producers of information, goods and services put more emphasis on visual appeal in product design, advertising, marketing and television. Median earnings for salaried visual artists who usually work full time were about $20,000 a year in 1988. The middle fifty percent earned between $15,000 and $28,000 a year. The top ten percent earned more than $37,000.

Actors, Directors and Producers--Actors entertain and communicate with people through their interpretation of dramatic roles. They rely on facial and verbal expression as well as body motion for creative effect.

Directors interpret plays or scripts. Directors use their knowledge of acting, voice and movement to achieve the best possible performance and usually approve the scenery, costumes, choreography and music.

Producers select plays or scripts and hire directors, principal members of the cast and key production staff members. Producers also coordinate the activities of writers, directors managers, and other personnel, arrange financing and decide on the size of the production and its budget.

In 1988, actors, directors and producers held an average of about 80,000 jobs in motion pictures, state plays, television and radio.

These are just a few of the avenues of opportunities open to all people. A key factors in creating, establishing and maintaining success in our lives is creativity and flexibility with our eyes and hearts wide open to the life given to us.

In that blacks are extremely weak in the area of businesses owned, blacks should consider starting businesses in all areas., i.e, grocery stores, cleaners, drug stores, car washes, real estate agencies, banks, credit unions, restaurants, hotels, gas stations, book stores, distribution networks, manufacturing, newspapers, furniture stores, travel agencies, automotive repair shops, employment agencies, vocational schools, credit unions, print shops, malls, movie theaters, music studies, film studies, etc., the opportunities are unlimited. We are only limited by our own lack of vision, imagination and laziness.

SUGGESTED READING

Live Your Dreams
By Les Brown
Million Dollar Habits
By Robert J. Ringer
Trump Surviving At The Top
By Donald J. Trump
Think And Grow Rich
A Black Choice
*By Dennis Kimbro
and Napoleon Hill*
Unlimited Power
By Anthony Robbins
You Can Have It All
By Arnold M. Patent
We're Number One
By Andrew L. Shapiro
Entrepreneuring-The Ten
Commandments For Building A
Growth Company
By Steven C. Brandt
How To Plan And Finance A
Growing Business
Edited by Donald M. Dible
Thrive On Stress
By Dr. Robert Sharpe & David Lewis
184 Businesses Anyone Can Start And Make
A Lot Of Money
The Editors of Entrepreneur
How To Really Create A Successful Marketing
Plan *David E. Gumpert*

Bibliography

An Empak "Black History" Publication Series, *A Salute to Black Civil Rights Leaders."*

Barson, Michael, *When You're Doing Better Than He Is*, Cosmopolitan, January 1991

Bureau of Labor Statistics, *Occupational Outlook Handbook 1990-91 Edition.* U.S. Department of Labor, April 1990

Ebony Magazine, *The Legacy of Thurgood Marshall "The Best I Could With What I Had"*

Ellin, Nancy *Notable Black Women* Michigan Department of Education-Office For Sex Equity. January 1984

Ross Perot, *Ross Perot Speaks out & United We Stand*

Gatewood, Andrew R. *The social and Economic Status of Young Black Males and the Impact on the Formation of Detroit Area Black Families.* United Community Services of Metropolitan Detroit. August, 1989

Givens, Robin, *Why Are Black Actresses Having Such a Hard Time in Hollywood?* Ebony, June, 1991

Johnson, Bill, *City Leaders Fail to Address Culture of Violence* Detroit News, Editorial Notebook, January 10, 1992

Mathis, Renita, *Black Inventors*, Upscale Magazine, February/March 1992

Sister Mary Rose McGeady, *God's Lost Children*, Covenant House, 1991

Mathis, Renita, *Black Inventors, Upscale Magazine*, February/March 1992

The Detroit News, *The Suicide Gap*, Source: National Center for Health Statistics

Palmer, Leslie, Lena Horne-Entertainer, Published by Grolier Incorporated 1990-1989

The Detroit News, *Letterman Books (Potato(e) Kid,* by Fred Pieretti, Associated Press

Woodroofe, Debby, Sisters In Struggle 1848-1920

The Detroit Free Press, June 11, 1992. *Gap Widens For Races*, Dan Gillmore--Free Press Staff Writer

Leslau, Charlotte and Wolf, *African Proverbs*

The Reader's Digest Association, *The Last Two Million Years*

Bennett, Lerone Jr., *Before The Mayflower*

Terry,Ted, *American Black History*

Hacker, Andrew, *Two Nations*

Wright, John W., General Editor, *The Universal Almanac*

Hoffman, Mark S., *The World Almanac*

Waitley, Denis Dr., *The Psychology of Winning*

Ringer, Robert J., *Million Dollar Habits*

Carruth, Gorton, *What Happened When-An Essential Collection of Facts & Dates From 986-Today*

Ebony Magazine, *The Year of the Black Woman* October, 1992

NO MORE ANGER!

NO MORE HATE!

NO MORE VIOLENCE!

...NO MORE PAIN!!!

<u>PEACE!</u>